Entirety

Entirety

LOVE GIVES ALL

DANA CANDLER

---

* Adapted from *St. Bernard of Clairvaux On the Song of Songs IV*, p. 186 (Cistercian Publications Inc., 1980).

DEDICATION

To my Husband, Matthew

Your deep hunger to be *wholly God's* continually strengthens and provokes me in love, bringing me back like an anchor to the sacred vows. Once again, it was you who made a way for me to write. Joyfully and skillfully taking over with our kids on one side, you were my constant encouragement on the other, continually processing these truths with me in our shared yearning for this message to be written on our hearts. This book is our heart's cry together, our deep prayer unto the Lord. May we give Him *everything*, day by day, with a holy love and sobriety…until the day we see His face. All my love.

And to my Daughter, Madison Clairvaux

May Jesus so win your heart by His love that even in your childhood and youth, you would be as one who shines with the Light of Love eternal. In the words of Bernard of Clairvaux, may you love Jesus with your whole being and therein lack nothing.

Contents

$\mathscr{F}$OREWORD

What exactly is God looking for? This question is most often neglected and avoided in our preaching, our counseling, our songwriting, and even in our daily lives. Yet it *must* be answered. We cannot evade it or get around it but must face it directly and wrestle with it until we embrace the answer. In *Entirety*, Dana points us to the *answer* of what God seeks from our lives—*hearts equally yoked in love.* God wants our full abandonment and nothing less, just as He Himself has given *all* for us.

We were made for the exhilaration of *free-falling* as we let go of our momentary security and fall into His infinite embrace. The more you've touched what it feels like to love God with your *everything*, the *more* you will want to give Him. In my own life, I have found myself actually *craving* the feeling of abandonment unto God. We were truly made for it. The more we die to ourselves and throw ourselves into the Father's will, as He prepares us for His Son, the more we will want to do it again and again! So compelling is this way of living that we will find ourselves actually looking for new bridges to burn, further things to give up, more areas to yield to God in. We will grow to love the romance of *leaving all behind* in order to cling to Him in greater measure.

I have known Dana for several years and have seen her *live for love* day after day, year after year, as so few do, giving herself unreservedly to God in the simplicity of everyday life. She knows that the answer to what God is looking for is not found in external positions or so-called success but in loving God entirely.

I highly recommend *Entirety* to you, and I believe that as you read this book you will be moved to love the Lord your God with all that you are in the midst of all that you do.

—*Misty Edwards*
Worship Leader, Int'l House of Prayer of Kansas City

If we love with our "whole being, nothing is lacking where everything is given." —Bernard of Clairvaux

Chapter 1

OVE OF ENTIRETY

Bernard of Clairvaux has said well that we love less than God loves because we *are* less, but if we love with our whole being, *"nothing is lacking where everything is given."** Yes, Bernard is right. I am less than my Creator in every way, and my love for God is weak in that I am weak and broken. And thus it might seem that I could never share in love with the God who is Himself *perfect Love*. How is it then that the human heart, small and weak, could ever love the One who is all-powerful, holy, and perfect? How can we, the created, find communion and fellowship with the Creator? Where is the line in which these two loves—the love of God and the love of the believer—cross paths and intersect?

---

* *St. Bernard of Clairvaux On the Song of Songs IV*, p. 186 (Cistercian Publications Inc., 1980).

The answer lies in the title of this book—*Entirety*. Jesus' giving of His life for all has both *made a way* for me to love Him fully and also *demonstrated* how such a yielding is offered (1 Jn. 3:16; 4:19). As He gives His life entirely, He invites me to give *my* life entirely, and in this mutual emptying, there is great convergence. Herein, we find the union of God and man.

The love that the Lord *gives* and the love that He *wants* finds its unique quality and marked stamp in the fact of its *utter givenness*. The glory and essence of Love's nature, that which sets it apart from all else, happens in the laying down of one's life—the giving of oneself *entirely*. God has loved us with all that He is, emptying Himself in love to the uttermost, and though I am yet weak and broken, when I love Him in this *same* way, giving Him *all* that I am in the here and now, *nothing* is lacking where everything is given.

Holy Trembling

Entirety—to love the Lord with all the heart, soul, mind, and strength (Matt. 22:37). My heart feels the gripping of a holy trembling by the subject of loving God in this way. To love Him so wholly and with such unreservedness is something I long for, something He has ruined me with a high vision for, and yet something that requires nothing less than *everything*. *Entirety* comes at a high price, and by nature it rules out any exceptions.

As I write this book, I feel the trembling of knowing my own weakness, my own inability to hold true to a resolve unless He Himself fuels my fervency each step of the way. Yet all the while, I am gripped by a stunning vision: *God Himself has given all for love.* Is He not worthy of a love that matches His in its degree of yieldedness? How often the Lord is loved partially without being loved *unrestrainedly.* Yet what would it look like if there were a people, a generation, that burned in a fervency of love marked by a radical resolve to love Him in the way that He Himself loves—without restraint?

Jesus has extended an invitation to us of the highest order. It is a call to fervency that flows from the fullness of love. Just as His eyes pierced through the crowds of old, His gaze pierces our own hearts as His voice, laden with authority, cries out, "'You shall love the Lord your God with all your heart, with all your soul, and with all your mind'" (Matt. 22:37). With these words, Jesus summons the human heart out of its lethargy into wholehearted givenness to God. He beckons us to the only foreseeable future, the only *plausible* outlook, if we desire to live in the fullness of His highest for us. He calls us to give Him *everything.*

The truth is that we were *made* to abandon ourselves, made to give all in love without compromise. Innate in our makeup is dissatisfaction with half-heartedness and a yearning to love and be loved to the uttermost. It is the highest way to live, the most pleasurable and freeing existence for the human heart. The frustration we experience in apathy and the discontent we face in partiality is not something within us gone awry but rather a cry lifting its voice that is holy and God-given. We were created with this groan for wholeheartedness because God Himself is wholehearted. He put within us the inescapable yearning for complete givenness so that we would grope with a holy restlessness whenever full yieldedness is not intact.

Present Tense Wholeheartedness

To love the Lord with all that I am—to give Him *everything*—how I've known the words and felt their wrenching invitation upon my heart in my own life. Through the years, a thousand times have I set my heart over and over again in the pursuit of loving God fully. This commandment has been to me of most precious worth, the first and highest—the call to love Him with all that I am. Yet ever so subtly some false notions concerning such a way of living were present.

Without realizing it, I most often perceived the fulfillment of these vows made unto the Lord to be something somewhere off in my future, the destiny I am headed for, yet not the place I am currently living. Aware of my shortcomings, my weaknesses, and my yet immature love for Him, the dream of truly loving Him with *all of my heart*—carried out in all of my actions, my time, my thoughts, my relationships, my finances, etc.—seemed to be impossible in the present tense. To be wholehearted for God seemed too distant a realization for *right now,* not a place I might experience presently, in all the ordinary days of my journey and the difficulties of my less-than-perfect pursuit. It was a distant dream and a faraway shore to which I was headed, in which I longed to live, yet was still a long ways off. It was to me a place I yearned for, the place I set my heart to reach for, knowing that one day I would arrive there, perhaps at the end of my years, when finally I reached the heights of mature love. All of these perceptions I held in the subtle recesses of my understanding until recently…when my belief that wholehearted love unto God was presently unobtainable changed in my understanding to become absolutely *reachable* and undeniably *accessible*.

It was not very long ago, at the close of an ordinary day filled with all the common parts of life that any mom with two children two and under might experience. My husband Matt and I were taking the long, extended, victorious sigh that we take every night after we get the kids to bed and at last experience those first initial moments of pure, uninterrupted quiet and stillness. *Ahhhhh.* It was in the lingering sigh that Matt said a simple yet profound statement. It surprised me and went in like an arrow to my heart, forever marking me with its impact. He said, *"You know…we can be wholehearted before God right now."*

Suddenly, this simple statement changed everything for me. A light went on in a place I did not know was darkened, and for the first time I believe I could see the shoreline that I thought was so far away. The distant dream of wholehearted living—of loving God with all my heart, soul, mind, and strength—was instantly not far off in the horizon but blazing before my eyes; I was face to face with it. It was then that a new understanding entered my heart, that loving God wholly is not something done or something offered once and for all. Nor is it just a vow made in the heightened moments of sincere desire—delayed in its fruition until the end of one's life—but rather an offering given unto God a thousand times a thousand, day after day after day. It is a posture of heart we can live in not eventually but presently, not in the culmination of years but in the presentation of moments, thousands upon thousands of small snatches of time and life offered in love unto God. Offering Him my everything throughout the day, holding nothing back, and restraining in no way comprise the very love that He is after—the love that He gave all to receive from me.

This way of life, the practice of giving God *our all*, is not too mysterious or far off that we cannot attain to it each and every day (Deut. 30:11, 14). It is something we live and experience not in general seasons of life but in moments, not in years, but in seconds—small flashes of wholehearted living. We so often would think He is waiting for that pinnacle day of spiritual maturity when we will finally reach wholehearted love for Him. Rather, He is looking for an absolute yieldedness in every area of our lives *today and right now*. If we give Him all today, then today, we lack nothing in love.

My life has been revolutionized by understanding I do not have to wait for a future day to be fully yielded to God. I can love Him with my all even today. Equally, I do not have to wait for heightened spiritual events to abandon myself unto God. Rather, I can love Him fervently through the ordinary and mundane parts of life. Love amidst the common is actually *exactly* what He asks of me. And this is the truth that I hope to bring to you in this book. To the classic subject of *God's love* for us and *our love* for Him, comes the crucial understanding of both the self-emptying *nature* of what this love requires, and the day to day *context* of where this love transpires.

We will begin in Part One of this book with considering this love of God—how He loves wholly and entirely—both in the love shared within the Godhead and the love poured out unto us. This love is the primal Source of all. Only from this great Source can we progress to Part Two of the book—our love, both for God and others. We love because He first loved, and as we become ruined in a holy way by His unrestrained love, we in turn will give ourselves to love Him in the same way—*entirely.*

PART ONE:

God's Love

CHAPTER 2

OVE OF THE TRINITY

"'...for You loved Me before the foundation of the world.'" Jn. 17:24

Long before you and I were born, before all the generations that have gone before us, way before Adam walked the earth, and before the world was formed was the Beginning of all beginnings—the Godhead, Three in One. If we could see beyond the boundary lines of this age, before the tickings of time were set in motion, our searchings would find the Origin of all foundations, the Source of all fountains—the God of perfect Love, holy and glorious.

Love within the Godhead

Have we *considered* what kind of love has dwelt for all eternity in the holy circle of Love Himself—between Father,

Son, and Holy Spirit? What does love look like when it is void of imperfection, when it holds no brokenness or frailty of fallenness?

From everlasting, far beyond the scope of where the human mind can stretch, the Father has loved the beloved Son, the express image of Himself, with ardent and perfect affection. Long before time came into existence, inconceivably longer than our minds can fathom, the Son has continually erupted with exploding love for His Father. And the Holy Spirit, the One who is the very breath of the Godhead, has loved Father and Son with incomprehensible zeal and jealousy, just as also the Father and Son have loved the Spirit of God with depths descending and heights mounting into infinity.

Delighting with all delights and enjoying with all pleasure, the Three Persons of the Trinity have shared in love perpetually from eternity—a whirlwind of tumultuous affections, pure as God is pure and consuming as God is all-consuming (Deut. 4:24; Jn. 1:1; 17:5, 24; Prov. 8:22–31).

Love's Nature: Giving All

God *is love* and this we know, but before you and I were brought into the knowing of this God that we love, this God that has first loved us, He *was love* from everlasting. He was love from before time. Love unending and love all-consuming. And this love, that was Himself, was a billowing violent flow between Father, Son, and Spirit. Love unyielding,

14

unwavering, untiring, and unrelenting. And though our minds are fractured and frail and our hearts distant and far, though we know that this eternal exchange is beyond our comprehension and surpassing our understanding, what we know in certainty of the *nature* of this love is that from eternity it is a love that pours itself out *wholly* and *entirely* (Eph. 3:19). We *know* and recognize love by the face that it always wears, the essential quality that it always exudes: the laying down of itself on behalf of another (1 Jn. 3:16).

Always has the Father loved the Son with a love that is *entire*, and forever without beginning has the Son loved the Father with a wholeness void of fractions. When God the Word was with God the Father, hidden in His bosom in the beginning—*towards* Him in continual communion and perpetual fellowship—it was a love of *utter givenness* and *complete yielding* one to another (John 1:1–2). Love Himself has loved within that great circle of the Holy Three—One in essence, three in Persons—with a pouring forth wholly and without reserve for all eternity.

Love of Father and Son

From eternity past, in that expanse beyond the beginning of time and surpassing the stretch of human understanding, what did it look like when God the Father loved God the Son? Though we can only peer with such limited perspective, with all certainty, we know that this was a love that could only rightly be described as *absolute* and *plentiful*, a love reserving nothing and offering everything. "'The Father loves the Son, and has given all things into His hand'" (Jn. 3:35).

Even before the Word became flesh and the Father sent forth Jesus, the plan in the Father's heart from everlasting was that He would withhold nothing from the only begotten Son, filling Him with all the fullness of the Godhead bodily (Col. 2:9). Finding great pleasure in total extravagance, His delight was to give all things into the hands of His Son and put all things under His feet (Eph. 1:22; Heb. 2:8). Truly, the love the Father had for the Son even before the worlds were formed was characterized by the giving of His all unto the Son. *This giving of His entirety is the expression and the perfection of love.* The Father gave all unto the Son from eternity. Withholding nothing. Giving everything. Perpetually and without end.

Jesus, the Beloved Son of the Father, Love Incarnate, has loved His Father in great extravagance—who from the foundations, before time began, became the slain Lamb, offering Himself in utter abandon unto the Supreme Source of All (Rev. 13:8). Before any other witness would peer in to the greatest self-emptying of all time, Jesus the Word declared unto the Father His abandonment even unto death in the words, "'Behold, I come; in the scroll of the book it is written of me. I delight to do Your will, O my God, and Your law is within my heart'" (Ps. 40:7–8).

Being in the form of God, Jesus did not consider it something to be grasped to be equal with God. He emptied

Himself of the privileges of dwelling with the Father in all glory and receiving the adorations of the heavenly hosts continually, and He took the form of a bondservant to the very point of death (Phil. 2:7–8). This was not a departing from His character but rather an action in perfect unity with who He was as God. In accord with His own nature, He withheld utterly nothing from His Father in the offering of the whole of Himself. He delighted to do His Father's will as His sustaining motivation and desire, even unto death, as He entrusted Himself into His Father's hands on the cross (Jn. 4:34; Lk. 23:46). All of this was love made manifest.

Utter Givenness

Conclusively, the beauty of love lies in the giving of all and withholding of nothing. Greater love has no one than the one who lays down his life utterly, pours out his possessions entirely, offers himself wholly to the one he loves (Jn. 15:13). The nature of the God of love from everlasting—both in the love shared within the Godhead and the love poured forth unto mankind— is found in its utter emptying of itself for another. It is not just that He has loved us in everlasting duration. It is not only that the quality of His affections is immeasurable, but that the *amount* of His love is *entire*.

God's love eternally is whole and without fraction. Everything is given and nothing withheld, distinguishing it from any lesser love in its highest purity. The highest love is demonstrated in the laying down of the whole of one's life for another (Jn. 15:13; 1 Jn. 3:16). The quality and nature that will forever and always set God's love apart from all lesser loves, the signature of its Source and the mark of its authenticity is found in its unyielding propensity to pour itself out utterly and completely.

Love Poured Forth unto Mankind

This same love, eternally alive in the Godhead, *the love of entirety*, has been given and poured out by God unto us. The love, with which the Father has loved the Son, and the Son unto the Father, wholly and freely without restraint, is the love that has pursued us wholly. Jesus said, "'As the Father loved Me, I also have loved you...'" and "'...that the world may know that You have sent Me and have loved them as You have loved Me,'" declaring blatantly that the very same love God had for the Son, He also possesses for us (Jn. 15:9; 17:23). This is a statement of unthinkable proportion. What kind of thunder struck through the heavenly hosts when the Son of God uttered these most staggering words, declaring God has loved you and I with the very same love that He has loved His only begotten Son?!

No need or lack has ever existed in this holy eternity of communion—this eternal pouring out between Father, Son, and Spirit. No arising vacancy or void has ever voiced its deficiency. For all is summed up in God and in Him is all life, all light and all love. He knows no fault, no shortcoming, no inadequacy, and no insufficiency. In Himself there is no absence but only presence, no vacancy but only fullness. He is the Eternally Rich One, the One who is Himself all fulfillment. It was out of this perfect wholeness that God created humanity—not to fill a void in Himself, but to share His fullness. Creating mankind in His image, He carved within every human soul the yearning to be loved wholly and to love wholly, even the capacity to love Him with the very same love He has loved us (Jn. 17:26). Thus, He destined to bring the living thirst of the human spirit into the Fountain of Living Waters.

Somewhere in the depths of God's being, He has reserved room for this ordained desire—the desire that He would bring unfulfilled mankind into the Answer of Himself, the perfection of His own Love. The Creator desires to bring the created into the communion shared between Father, Son, and Holy Spirit. His determined desire is to bring us into the fullness of His embrace, the plentitude of love within the Godhead.

The idea that we have been invited into the sharing and the fellowshipping of *God's own intimacy* seems preposterous and appalling if we have considered it rightly—for it is just so. When the Gospel is preached rightly, it has always caused unjust men to fall aghast at so great an entrance, so grandiose a gift, so baffling a report. It has always caused self-righteous men to cry, "Heresy," at so great a mercy, so perplexing a stooping of the God of Heaven, so scandalous a sacred story as the One who was rich, becoming so poor, that He might indeed bring us into His own wealth, His own peace and fellowship with the Father.

Invited into Love's Fullness

He has chosen to make us participants in this fellowship, that we would know and experience this holy exchange. By the voluntary response of our hearts, He has willed that we would enter into a role of non-passive participation, that we ourselves would love Him in the way He has always loved, and from our own hearts would arise an abandonment unto God that is of the same nature of His abandonment to us. From the beginning God has made His intentions clear. *He wants us to love Him with all our heart, soul, mind, and strength even as He has always and eternally loved us in this way* (Deut. 30:6; Matt. 22:37).

When Jesus proclaimed the first commandment, He knew well the *holy groping* for wholeheartedness in the human heart—a cry originating from the hand and will of the Creator. For He was beside the Father at creation, delighting in forming the sons of men, as this inherent groaning for fullness was lodged deep in each one's soul (Prov. 8:30). Jesus' timeless call for the *entirety* of the human heart is aimed directly at this yearning He placed in us. His charge is issued out of the truth of love's nature—love's demand for *all* and its refusal of half-heartedness. God does not love inside boundaries or up to a certain point, but fully. And this is how He invites us to love Him and to love others, with the very same love (Jn. 17:26).

For those of us that might have heard this beckoning of God in the first commandment with any tinge or tenor of harshness—if this command has approached our hearts with a feeling of being too difficult, too hard or too extreme—we have yet to understand the Person behind the plea, the heart behind the appeal. How much has the Father loved us in the giving of His only Son to us? How far has the Son descended in the taking on of our very frame and flesh and giving His life for us unto death? God bids us to love Him wholly, yes. But this bidding is laden with a love that has from all eternity poured out its *everything* for us.

CHAPTER 3

ℒOVE OF THE FATHER

"For God so loved the world that He gave His only begotten Son...."
Jn. 3:16

We know the above words well, perhaps too well, yet behind these words so well-known in many a Sunday school classroom are heartrending truths about the heart of God the Father, though distant from our understanding. Having looked at the love within the Godhead as Three in One, now let us narrow in and focus our gaze upon the love and heart of the Everlasting Father and His giving of the Son unto us.

With just the three words, "that He *gave*," we will spend eternity in untiring gratitude and amazement. The truth of the Father's eternal love for you and I resounds like great thunder in the giving of His Son. It is not elementary to consider so vast a subject. It is not something to casually assume we already understand. What kind of love was demonstrated by the heart of the Father in the offering of His only Son (Rom. 5:8)? This understanding of His heart is indispensible to our spiritual lives. As our hearts are struck by the Father's surging love, we will be able to love Him with a full response (1 Jn. 4:19).

Love for the Son

Before the foundations of the world, the Father loved the Son, dwelling with Him in eternity past in perfect communion and fellowship, daily His delight, the Man who was His Companion (Jn. 1:1–2; 17:24; Prov. 8; Zech. 13:7). In the midst of His High Priestly prayer as Jesus faced the cross momentarily—lifting His beloved friends to His Father—Jesus drew upon that recollection from eternity past, the remembrance that no other human being has ever possessed to draw upon. He prayed, "'And now, O Father, glorify Me together with Yourself, with the glory which I had with you before the world was…for You loved Me before the foundation of the world" (Jn. 17:5, 24). He recalled the ways and the expressions of how His Father loved Him before His assumption of a human frame—a holy, eternal exchange of affection that preceded His entrance into the world as a babe in a manger.

How great the love of the Father for His beloved Son—His only begotten One, this One in whom was all His delight from everlasting, His express image, God of God and

Light of Light. How unutterable the rendering in the offering of His most precious and most beloved One. How wrenching the depths of His own Person, how unspeakable the giving, and how telling the Story of Love in so great a Gift.

In the offering up of His own Son, the Father spared nothing and bestowed everything. He reached into His deepest parts—the unknown regions, the unsearchable and uncharted—and He rent His heart. He ripped of His own depths and drew out of Himself in the utmost act of giving, the highest rendering of offering, the deepest displaying of sacrifice ever to be demonstrated—He gave of His *only* (Jn. 3:16).

The Great Giving

We do not know what God has done—how far He has gone, how great He has given—in the giving of His Son. Love Himself, the Father of all, has given everything, sparing nothing. As in the story of Abraham, when God asked him to sacrifice his *only* son, the son he loved, our Heavenly Father gave of His *only*, the Son of His love, the only begotten (Gen. 22:2). All the Father's promises were wrapped up in Him, the Holy Seed (Gal. 3:13–16).

With love unimaginable for a people still His enemies, the Father offered up the One "in whom are hidden all the treasures of His wisdom and knowledge" (Rom. 5:10; Col. 2:3). He drew out of the bowels of His eternal being and spared not that which He held most precious, most costly, most beloved. He delighted to put within Jesus the fullness of the Godhead and in so doing gave of His whole being unto us in the sending of Jesus to the world (Col. 2:9). In the giving of His only Son, He gave *all* without reserve (Rom. 8:32; Jn. 3:16).

We see illustration of this unreserved giving of the Father in Jesus' parable about the man who planted a vineyard and then went away for an extended time (Lk. 20:12–14). After leaving His vineyard in the hands of some tenants, this Great Vineyard Owner, depicting the heavenly Father, sent servant after servant on His behalf back to the tenants.

This exemplifies how from the dawning of time, the Father has always given in every way with arms outstretched and desire evident. From the daily declaration of the rising sun to the utterance of every calling of creation making Him known, to the proclamation of every prophet of old—He has never been silent in His reach (Rom. 1:19–20).Yet as the parable portrays, these servants that He sent were not *headed* by the tenants of His vineyard. Many were even hated, beaten, and killed.

And so, in the fullness of time, after sending servant after servant and witness after witness, the Father gave the ultimate sacrifice. He gave of His *only*. He sent forth His beloved, begotten Son. He poured forth entirely and without lack, as if to say, "Now will I demonstrate My own love. Now will I display the essence of who I am. Now will My love be made fully known." As John the Apostle concludes, "In this the love of God was manifested toward us, that God sent His only begotten Son into the world, that we might live through Him" (1 Jn. 4:9).

Love Indescribable

Who is like our beloved God? Who would do what He has done, give as He has given, and sacrifice as He has sacrificed? It is unthinkable to us, completely foreign to our views and our ways. Who would give his only one, his beloved one, his most precious, over to those who were yet enemies, those who were far off (Rom. 5:10; Eph. 2:13)? There is *no one* who would give such an offering, *no one* who would pay such a price. Such a love is completely unfamiliar to man. We do not know nor recognize it.

God's offering and sacrifice is so counter to our nature, so opposing to our pride, so challenging to our comfort zones. He is God, and we are not like Him. He is love, and except He brings us into that very surging of His own love and illumines our darkened understanding, we have no comprehension of it, no overlap of knowledge, no reference point of recognition. Unless He gives us entrance into the love that is His own and none other's, man remains in remoteness, an uncomprehending spectator of an incomprehensible story. Unless one knows *Him*, he cannot know love because the only way to know love is to know God—the One who *is* Love. The one who does not love has not yet known and experienced

God—for the only entrance into love is through the knowledge of the One who *is* Love. "He who does not love does not know God, for God is love" (1 Jn. 4:8).

If one has not been enlightened by the love of God, His story in the Gospel—the greatest drama of all of Time's unfolding—is a sheer scandal if not a complete disgrace or an offensive outrage. What has God the all-powerful and all-knowing *done* in the sending forth of His own Son into utter poverty and complete obscurity, into total frailty and absolute dependency? This One who was His only Son He tore from heaven's glory with a ripping that forever revealed His heart, demonstrating His own love through the sending of this Jesus to mankind (Rom. 5:8).

The love of the Father was demonstrated not only in the *sending* of Jesus but in the *context* of which He came, the *climax* of His days being the cross. It was not as a king all-powerful, not as a ruler insurmountable that the Father sent His Son, but rather, this most cherished One came to us in the form of a baby so in need, to a family poor and unknown. He was wholly reliant on a weak mother and father, totally shrouded in hiddenness, with a life-plan culminating off the comprehensible charts. The Father's plan for His Son from before the foundations of the world was that of a cross, that of a sacrifice unimaginable and a death so appalling that men would look away from Him horrified and hide their faces in scorn (Is. 53:3; Rev. 13:8).

Not Distant from the Story

As I consider this *great giving* of the Father, I am moved by meditating upon what must have transpired in His own heart, knowing all things, through the stages of Jesus' life and death. I imagine, when He sent the angels to proclaim the glory of His Son's entrance onto the scene of our story, how He must have rejoiced with joy insurmountable as they sang, "Glory to God in the highest," knowing fully what this entrance would ultimately lead to—His eternal plan to bring the created order into fellowship with Himself (Lk. 2:14; Jn. 17:24). Yet this real rejoicing in His heart as the eternal Father was not without the anguish of also knowing the determined future of that precious Baby. Even as Mary held the Christ Child for the first time, looking into His eyes with a wonder so extraordinary, the Father in Heaven knew the sword that would eventually pierce through her soul (Lk. 2:35). He was not distant from the story, and just as Mary's heart, frail in its humanity, would feel the sword of Jesus' suffering, how much *more* was the Heavenly Father's heart assailed by the great piercing of the suffering His Son would endure, the cross He would bear?

As I meditate on this giving of God, it seems far too fragmented of thinking to assume that, because the Father knew of Jesus' coming resurrection, He did not experience the severe suffering of heart in the tragedy of the torture and rejection that awaited His Son. Indeed, such a disconnect and distance would outrage us if any human father were to share in his son's sufferings so indifferently. We would deem it unthinkable for a father to feel anything less than absolute anguish if he held his newborn son knowing all the while that a horrendous future awaited him.

Considering these things, we are brought back to the great question, the great inquiry: O God, what have You done in the sending of Your only Son? What has Your heart undergone in committing this One that You loved so eternally, so unrestrainedly, to become as a Lamb led to the slaughter (Is. 53:7)? We must be brought to the concluding consideration of what this display of divine giving tells us of God's love for mankind. If the Father loved the only begotten Son so immeasurably from all eternity, if He cherished Him with such incomprehensible depth of affection, what does His giving of Him on our behalf speak of the vastness of His love for *us*?

This is Love

This giving of God's *only* was the proclamation of His love for us, the telling and the rendering of His affections. It stands forever as the demonstration of the magnitude of His love for humanity. The cross has become for all time the apex of God's revealing of His deep love for weak and broken human beings. John declares, "In this is love, not that we loved God, but that He loved us and sent His Son to be the propitiation for our sins" (1 Jn. 4:10).

Because of His great love with which He loved us, He made us alive together with Christ while we were yet in our trespasses, delivering us from the power of darkness, conveying us into the Kingdom of the Son of His love, and exhibiting forever the heights and depths of this all-consuming and undeserved love (Eph. 2:4–5; Eph. 3:18; Rom. 5:8; Col. 1:13).

Oh, to not be dull and distant from that which causes the angels and heavenly hosts to still shutter and tremble, that which will cause our own hearts to fall aghast again and again, ten-thousand times ten-thousand for all the eternal ages to come. "Behold what manner of love the Father has bestowed on us, that we should be called children of God!" (1 Jn. 3:1).

As the Father has loved us from everlasting, so too has the Son. In the same way that the Father has given everything in the giving of His Son, the Son has given entirely in the giving of His life. Just as indispensible as the meditation of the Father's love is the love of the Son.

CHAPTER 4

*L*OVE OF THE SON

*"'...the Son of God, who loved me and gave Himself up
for me.'" Gal. 2:20*

We know and think of Jesus from our first sight of
Him, a helpless Baby lain in a manger in an environment so
primitive and crude. We recall the stories of His youth, how
He taught in the synagogue and how He grew in wisdom and
favor with God and man (Lk. 2:52). We know Him later in His
ministry to the masses, His teachings and His healings, His
words of profound authority and weight, His compassion and
demonstrations of love unparalleled—ultimately culminating
in a cross of utter self-giving, the supreme symbol of love, the
image of the greatest offering ever given.

When we think of Jesus, we begin with these images
and these conceptions, for this is how He first revealed

Himself to us. Yet there is more to His story than the frail beginnings of Bethlehem, and unless we push back that curtain to the scenes before the shepherds and kings to that which preceded the angelic host on Bethlehem's hillside, we will not know the unutterable greatness and scandalous entrance of this One who gave Himself unto those who were once His enemies—the One who laid down His life, His all, not just in part but in *entirety*.

Eternality of Jesus

Jesus, the Living Word, was God from eternity, begotten before time, dwelling in the unapproachable light with the Father, inhabiting the everlasting ages before the world was made in all glory and majesty (Jn. 1:1–2). Perpetually worshipped by angels, He possessed all things from all eternity, and to any onlooker of the adoring heavenly hosts, there was no apparent reason for this to change.

Yet in the heart of God, from this love of the Holy Three, there was a plan of *scandalous* proportions rooted in *outrageous* love, and the crux of that plan involved the unthinkable departing of the Begotten Son from the shrouds of unapproachable light and the unimaginable emptying of Himself in the assumption of a human frame. It meant the unthinkable mystery that God *the Creator* would enter the world through the womb of a young maiden whom *He Himself* created, and ultimately, the shocking culmination of *God* hanging on a cross—the eternal statement of His endless *hatred* of sin and everlasting *love* of mankind.

The Baby that we find in the manger was the same One who was eternally the Possessor of All, the Author of Life, the uncreated One who was with God from everlasting (Mic. 5:2). He did not consider His eternal exaltation as something to be grasped and used for His own gain, but rather He chose in transcendent love to empty Himself of so great an exaltation, making Himself of no reputation and taking on the form of a bondservant (Phil. 2:6–7).

Out of the erupting love and desire of the Godhead, the Son left the covering of unapproachable light and the vastness of His heavenly riches, wrapping Himself in the profound obscurity of poor humanity and becoming to the natural eye nothing more than a newborn Jewish boy, and later a typical young man, son of a carpenter, from Nazareth. In these obscure, ordinary beginnings, the extraordinary occurred: God took on the plight of humanity, the weakness and frailty of our dilemma and forever assumed His identity as our *Brother*, making us bone of His bone and flesh of His flesh forever.

Descent of Love

Descending to the dire need of estranged humankind, the unthinkable transpired, and the One who was rich became poor (2 Cor. 8:9). The One who had everything embraced having nothing. The One who knew incessant adoration by the lauding of all the angels and heavenly hosts welcomed the form of the nameless, the unknown, the poor and unrenowned. And having embraced this poverty that struck at the heart of Heaven with unmatched force, His descent did not cease even there. When the angels watched in wonder and astonishment at how Jesus the Creator and Ruler of All could descend so low, *lower still* did love compel Him in a living movement of meekness from highest heights to lowest depths.

Having assumed the poverty of the human plight in the incarnation, Jesus plunged yet still deeper into the piercing heart of humility, becoming obedient to His Father in a surrender that blazed with holy love. Lower, lower, lower did He go unto the point of death on the cross (Phil. 2:8). This descent was in no way a departing from His essence; He was not acting in a way contrary to His nature. Rather, He was the exact representation of the attributes of God (Heb. 1:2–3). With every lowering was a louder expression of that which has always been true of Him—a greater revealing of what God is like. Drinking the full cup His Father prepared for Him, Jesus demonstrated this nature of God by enduring the greatest suffering and death for the sake of love and the saving of our souls (Heb. 12:1–2; 5:8; Phil. 2:8).

From before the foundations of the world, the Lamb was slain out of the fueling ardent flame of love in God's heart (Rev. 13:8). It was this eternal flame that was revealed in the incarnation and crucifixion. In the heart of the Son was a love so compelling and so gripping, motivating every movement of His self-lowering and self-descent. For joyful love unto His Father and joyful love unto you and me, He endured the cross (Heb. 12:2). In Jesus' giving of Himself, the hidden plan of God's heart was revealed in the midst of time and space, and Love was the message made manifest. Because He cherished us, Christ fulfilled the requirements of God's justice to span the total disparity between God and man. In love, He reached for us in a way He alone could, closing the chasm that was otherwise irreparable. Through Christ's death, offered in love transcendent, He "washed us from our sins in His own blood" (Rev. 1:5).

He Gave All

Jesus poured Himself out in love unto us, giving Himself up utterly for us, not just in the giving of His physical life unto death, but in the free offering of all of His excellencies, His beauties, His preciousness, and His own righteousness. Indeed, the essence of His whole being He has entrusted to us, pouring into us the very Spirit by which He breathes (Gal. 1:4; 2:20; Eph. 5:25; Tit. 2:14).

When He gave us entrance into His own inheritance, it is not as though He drew a line in the sand and said, "Thus far and no more." Rather, He opened wide the riches of His glory and said to all those who are His, "All that I have is yours" (Jn. 16:15). He gave everything and no less, joining us to Himself in oneness and, in so doing, giving us entire access to all that He has (Jn. 1:16; Eph. 5:30–32). As co-heirs with Christ, we are invited to live in the same intimacy He has with the Father and to experience the reality that He has gladly chosen to share all things with us (Rom. 8:17; 1 Cor. 3:21–22).

This offering of Christ's *all* has become our reference point for love; it is the way in which we know and recognize its face and its manifestation (1 Jn. 3:16; 4:9). In the pouring out of His soul unto death, love was given an eternal depiction, as if God the Father, who is Love, were to say for all eternity, "Look upon this rendering of My affections and *therein* come to recognize My love."

Surely, I do not know the depths of the death that Jesus embraced. Nor do I know the greatness of His self-emptying, giving His all, down to the last drop (Eph. 5:2; Phil. 2:8). The heart of the Lamb gave in a giving that we have not fathomed and in so doing *loved* with a demonstration surpassing knowledge (Eph. 3:16–19).

We say that we want to love Him, and one of the first ways we do this is to consider with loving devotion what He has eternally given in the gift of Himself. We must take that familiar cross to our hearts and meditate upon it day and night, until the dullness that we know is replaced with a sacred devotion—until we can begin to see, with hearts flooded anew in love, why this Cross stands at the center of human history, the climax of our story, the focal point of Love for all the ages (Song of Sol. 1:13).

Burdened by the weighty love extended in the cross, Saint Alphonsus Liguori stated:

> *If people would only stop to consider, looking at Jesus on the cross, the love that he has borne each one of them! "With what love," says Saint Francis de Sales, "would we not be set ablaze at the sight of those flames in the Redeemer's breast! And oh, what happiness, to be able to be burned by that same fire with which our God burns for us! What joy, to be bound to God by the chains of love!" Saint Bonaventure called the wounds of Jesus Christ wounds that cut through the most senseless hearts, and which inflame the most frigid souls. How many arrows of love come forth from those wounds, to strike the hardest hearts! What flames issue from the burning heart of Jesus Christ, setting on fire the coldest souls! And how many chains come from that wounded side to bind the most rebellious hearts!* [*]

He Invites Me to Give All

When the piercing eyes of Jesus address me and beseech me to love Him with all of my mind, heart, soul, and strength, He asks of me only what He Himself has already given (Matt. 22:37). He wants *my everything* for *His everything, my all* for *His all, my entirety* for *His entirety*. From the heights of

---

[*] St. Alphonsus Liguori, *The Practice of the Love of Jesus Christ*, p. 7 (Ligouri Publications, 1997).

Heaven's adoration, with glory and light and power, He stooped down so low, so heartrendingly low. With this understanding of how *He* has emptied Himself for love, His highest command rings in my heart with the deep undertones of His own obedience of this same command. He invites me to keep His commandments just as He Himself has kept His Father's commandments, calling them good and not burdensome (Jn. 15:10; 1 Jn. 5:3). He asks with that deep acquaintance and familiarity of having already climbed this mountain Himself, only His was a scaling of radical heights and extreme depths that no man has ever known.

With all His heart, soul, mind, and strength has He loved from everlasting, and while on the earth as He walked out His life, He loved to this same degree. He does not ask me to do anything that He Himself has not already done, and thus His invitation holds within it the deep authority of His own embracing of its essence. He asks that I lay down my life in love even as He has laid down His. When His eyes meet mine, I am pierced by the beseeching born out of His own living experience with the request He gives. He *knows* what He asks.

How great the invitation Jesus has extended to us. In Part Two, we will look deeper into both His call and our response to entirety. For now, let us continue to consider the scandalous emptying of the Son of God and the great heart of meekness fueling His extravagance.

CHAPTER 5

*L*OVE EMPTIES

"'Greater love has no one than this, than to lay down one's life for his friends.'" Jn. 15:13

Love gives all and its very nature is to empty itself. In the giving of His life unto death, Jesus demonstrated His desire to give in fullness and not in part. He did not will to love within measure. He did not want to bless us from a distance but to *embrace* us in shared nearness. For love, Jesus has given *all*, embraced poverty, and emptied Himself.

The giving of Jesus' *all* is the Gospel that has become our own story—the Good News that has forever changed the course of who we were as former enemies of God, once in darkness, now children of the light (Eph. 5:8). He became our Brother, and in that becoming, we have been brought near to God (Eph. 2:13). It is through the door of His poverty or His self-emptying, His complete giving of Himself, that we have been given entrance into the extravagance of knowing God.

This mighty One who was in the beginning with God, inhabiting eternity in all glory and power, had to become our Brother in order for us to access Him (Heb. 2:17). In order for ones so ordinary and frail, so common and poor, to know God, He had to bow so low that He might bring us high. How great the consolation of the truth that He is our *Brother*. When assailed with accusation about His disinterest, His far-ness, or His disapproval, we may find great comfort in this identity that Jesus embraced. He is not ashamed to call us His (Heb. 2:11).

Deep Meekness and Chosen Poverty

At Jesus' first coming, the expectation and hope of the Jewish people was for a great King to come and overthrow all the enemies of God and set up His Kingdom in power on the earth—and rightly so, for this was the promise of the prophets (Num. 24:16–19; Isa. 9:6–7; 11:1–5ff.). The fact that Jesus came not to be served but to serve, not to ascend in honor but to descend in humility, not to conquer but to be killed, caused multitudes to reject Him and not receive Him as the true Messiah. Great was the stumbling block caused by the sheer meekness and poverty of the Son of God. Yet it was as though God was saying, "Receive My heart of meekness in order to receive *Me*. This is who I am, and it is your entrance into knowing Me."

One day He *will* come as the conquering King, and He *will* set up His throne in Jerusalem, subduing all of His enemies with power. Yet before this open display of might and power, He came in the poverty of His own emptying, with a rending exhibit of the deep meekness of God, an unthinkable espousing of our cause, and a perfect portrayal of the nature of Love in its drivenness to lay down its life.

Jesus is the only One who has ever *chosen* the poverty of being human. All mankind is born poor in his distance from God's manifest presence, his depravity, and his far-ness from glory. But *Jesus*, He was wholly wealthy from eternity without a touch of weakness or frailty—and He left this perfect prosperity in order to embrace an endless poverty in that forever He will remain in His humanity. All others besides Him were given something *greater* in their entrance into this world than they had before.

Every child of human history except Jesus, upon leaving of their mother's womb, gained greater capacity and opportunity than was theirs before. But before His mother's womb, Jesus was already rich beyond comprehension. His birth was not an arising or a gaining but an eternally severe stooping, a most astounding decreasing. And all of this marvelous movement from heights to depths in order that I, the commoner—I, the poor—might be brought through the door of His own poverty into the vast glory of His own inheritance.

This divine heart of meekness—of embracing the lowest place, of giving His life even unto death, entirely and not partially, wholly and without reserve—is the greatest demonstration of love ever established. It is the clear cry of what God has eternally been like. Though Jesus embraced poverty in His humanity, the meekness of His heart that fueled so great an emptying was eternally present. He lived forever in a heart of humility before the Father, and this was the heart-posture He expressed so vividly in the incarnation—the most extravagant expression of laying down His life. Here we see the most powerful depiction ever given of what love *is* and what love *does,* and it is our very point of entrance into knowing God and receiving of all that He has extended to us.

By nature we are not humble or meek but rather self-exalting and self-promoting. Christ's meekness becomes our "doorway" into His presence both by His own stooping to encounter us at the lowly level in which we live, and also by confronting our pride and self-absorption and directing us into humility. Meekness is the only meeting place for us to find encounter with God deeply. Thus He says to us, "'Blessed are the poor in spirit…blessed are the meek'" (Matt. 5:3, 5). The rule of His Kingdom is such that only as we humble ourselves in His sight will He lift us up (James 4:10). Therefore we see just how precious is this meekness of Christ—that which He possesses and that which He imparts. Meekness is so beyond a good quality to attain to. It is our only way forward in God.

His Meekness, My Entrance

What strikes me so much about this poverty of Jesus is how essential it is to my knowing of Him. Jesus joined Himself to us as our Brother, forever becoming the bridge that has closed the wide chasm between God and man. It is by this bridge that we find Him each day, through this poverty that we know Him and are known by Him. He is the High Priest that sympathizes with us in that He has walked our course and entered our sphere of living, and this fact is the reason we can know Him at all.

Unless He is gentle and lowly in heart, I truly have no hope in finding Him. Unless He is the One most meek and most humble, I've not a chance at knowing Him, for I am steeped in weakness and my life filled with all that is mundane and ordinary and common. My days are spent in many a monotonous activity, and only if He is the kind who can be found in the midst of such simplicity, do I have hope.

There is no other avenue to Him for me except His broken body and His humble heart. My only way of access is His poverty. If He is not poor as I am poor, then I have no doorway by which to enter His presence. If He is not my Brother, I will not ever be able to embrace Him. If He is any more mysterious than this, and the way to finding Him any more difficult, I've no hope in such a search. Only if He Himself is also a commoner, not distant or removed from such rudimentary life, but rather deeply acquainted and experiential-

ly familiar—only then is there a door of intimacy with Him
opened unto me.

The Meekest One

Jesus stands before us in His meekness, clothed in the
graying garments of humility, adorned in the weathered
wrappings of servanthood, having left His royal robes behind
in the emptying of Himself. It is in this humility so great that
so few even recognize Him. All these many centuries later
since His First Coming, and He still remains unknown and
unperceived, obscured in these garments that He gave everything to wear. His meekness somehow makes Him mysterious
to us, and His nearness to broken man leaves Him unfound by
most—too close to be sought in such proximity, too near to
be looked for in such closeness. Yet still, there He stands—so
invasively near, so overwhelmingly familiar. Overlooked by
most. Unrecognized by nearly all. Nothing about Him in this
frame draws men to Himself, no comeliness that we should
desire Him. In His magnitude of meekness, He stands with
arms outspread to all who would embrace Him in this
way...yet only to those and none other.

He has come not for the well but for the sick, not for
the full but for the hungry, not for the strong but for the weak,
not for the wise but for the simple. And these and no others
are those that find Him. For there is only one entrance into
knowing Him, and it is not the grand door that most would

imagine. It is not an entrance reserved only for the mighty, the gifted, and the clever. This dingy doorway is most often disregarded by any that truly do not know Him. To gain admittance, riches must be left behind. Favor and fame among men must be forgotten and chased no longer. The only way to find the real Jesus is to find Him where He is, where He has always been in the deepest, even darkest, places of eternal love. We find Him in the place where He emptied Himself and became poor.

Who would have known this mantle of meekness would so veil Him from being known? And for those who do find Him, that this would be the only window to peer through, the only doorway to find entrance? Those who have ever known Him knew Him first in meekness's manger—there and no other place. Anyone who has ever found Him came to see Him first in the dull light of His poorness, garbed in utter humility and decked in deep servanthood. Jesus refuses to be embraced or made known in any other way, saying to all who would come to Him, "The only way to gain access to the glories you were made for, to the riches that I have given everything to bring you into, is through My own poverty."

Surely, we find Him too close to be recognized. How could a King be found in such commonness? He is too near to be noticed, too available to be called upon. Truly, His nearness is our stumbling block. His proximity is our perplexity. We are commoners so lowly. Our homes are amidst the most mundane—in the deep caverns of the ordinary. We imagine our lives to be not the sort of places for a King to visit. With this perspective, we go about our business each day, doing the normal things of life while always looking out the windows of our walls of ordinariness and wondering when we will see Jesus. We dream of when we will catch a glimpse of the great King, when we might somehow reach Him if even in a far stretch—a slight touching of the mysterious place where He lives. Yet all of this searching out our windows is a vain exploration with a false expectation. He is not out there to be found. The King so great is not to be found in the mysterious realm so far away, distant and removed, for He has given everything and paid every price so as to not be so mysteriously far but rather inconceivably near. He has left an abode so high and plunged Himself so low. He is not in some distant land only to be accessed in our dreams. He has not left the ordinary but entered it, not neglected the lowly but embraced it. He is not outside our walls but within them, not beyond our windows but behind them. He is near. He is here. *Even now.*

This meekest One who has emptied Himself for us is truly profoundly present in the midst of our day-to-day lives. He desires that we find Him where He is and give Him our hearts in that place. His presence is not static but dynamic, as He reaches for us each day with a desire to encounter us. If we look for Him throughout our daily lives, we will not only find Him to be invasively present but also fervently in pursuit of us.

CHAPTER 6

*L*OVE PURSUES

"'And he who loves Me will be loved by My Father, and I will love him and manifest Myself to him.'" Jn. 14:21

The great story of God's self-giving and self-emptying would have been enough to convey how vast His eternal love for you and me was. Yet He sees fit to give even more manifestations of His love, yet more expressions of His affections through the encounters with His love that we find in the *present tense.* As we continue to look at the One who has loved us from everlasting, let us consider how He is also the One who loves us *currently,* in this small window of our everyday existence. The One who has given everything from all eternity— entirely in the giving of His Son, wholly in the offering of His own life—continues yet more in His extravagance by creating even more avenues to express His eternal love.

The God whose pursuit of me has been from the eternal ages is also the One who searches for me in the present-day, reaches for me in the beauties of creation and in the smallest of events of my circumstances, wanting to be found by me in the currency of the here and now. He waits to be found by any who will pursue and perceive Him. For anyone who is looking, He's actually *everywhere* and ever-present. This is our constant labor of devotion—to *look* for Love and to let our hearts be found by His continual reach.

Recognizing Love in Creation

The Lord's love is so extravagant, and though the crowning revelation of that extravagance was in the giving of His Son even unto death, He has continued His proclamation in a daily manner through the messengers of the created order. The natural order serves as a window into the supernatural, bringing any heart closer to the Creator if it but hears the message and beholds the beauty of the creation and the persistent announcement of the Creator's love behind it (Rom. 1:20).

David declares God's unrelenting pursuit of man through His messengers of creation:

> *The heavens declare the glory of God; and the firmament*
> *shows His handiwork. Day unto day utters speech, and*
> *night unto night reveals knowledge. There is no speech*
> *nor language where their voice is not heard. Their line*

has gone out through all the earth, and their words to the end of the world. In them He has set a tabernacle for the sun, which is like a bridegroom coming out of his chamber, and rejoices like a strong man to run its race. Its rising is from one end of heaven, and its circuit to the other end; and there is nothing hidden from its heat (Ps.19:1–6).

What was it that happened in the heart of David when as a young shepherd boy, buried in his present-tense monotony, God fed his hungry heart with the revelation that the sun was like a bridegroom? His ears were opened to hear the Creator's love-song: the unrelenting sunrise daily giving witness to a God who does not grow weary of loving His own but ever delights in His people as a bridegroom rejoices over his bride (Isa. 62:5)! How moved he must have been when this insight came like an arrow to his understanding. God wants to meet us in our present tense daily tasks just as He did David, even pursuing us by the created order, if we will only have eyes set on *seeing*. If we do not set our gaze to perceive and find His fingerprints, what is meant to be traces of the divine fascinating our hearts will remain as mere mechanics of life, lost and unperceived.

Many well-loved saints in history received the love of God extended to them in nature and the created order, perceiving the signs of the God of love all around and allowing their own hearts to be filled with burning love in response.

John of the Cross was a man who recognized creation as the visible theater in which God leaves traces of Himself for all those who will have eyes to see and be stirred in their devotion for Him, being brought deeper into His love. He wrote,

> *O woods and thickets,*
> *Planted by the hand of my Beloved!*
> *O green meadow, coated bright with flowers,*
> *Tell me, has He passed by you?**

Surely God has set the created order into motion as a continual witness, a voice that incessantly goes forth, a beauty that relentlessly exudes the message of His deep love and His extravagant kindness. He has not done this without the motivation of love burning in His heart and the yearning for the eyes of the hearts of men, who walk amidst this grandeur, to perceive love in all of this created life. Oh, to have ears to hear and eyes to perceive the heart of the Beloved behind this beauty!

Personalizing God's Pursuit in Creation

I'll never forget when I first believed that God was actually pursuing my heart with the mission of love in a *personal* manner through His created order. It happened for the first time with a flower...actually several of them. Over ten years

---

* St. John of the Cross, *The Collected Works of St. John of the Cross*, p 44 (ICS Publications, revised edition, 1991).

ago now, it's like yesterday in my memory. In those days, I lived with several girls in a duplex in a not-so-great part of town. Affordable? Yes. Safe? Well, let's just say that we were all glad to graduate from those times. Behind this duplex was what I called "my field." It was where I went to pray and be with God. In truth, it was an overgrown lot, a mess of weeds so thick that there was little draw for anyone to walk through it. Thus, it was mine, all mine. And in all of my trampings through my field, I never saw anyone else back there, only ever confirming to me that this was the place where God *waited* for me, the place He wanted to meet *me*.

It was one very hot day, as were most of the days spent in that field. I was pacing in prayer back and forth, up and down, sometimes with words, sometimes with a little song, sometimes with silence. I remember I wanted to make an actual visible path through those weeds that I could call my own, and so on this day, being not the first of the path-plowing endeavor, back and forth I walked in my trail, up and down in the same straight line, over and over and over and over again. This day was also like most others spent in this way in that there was not a lot happening in my prayer time in the perceivable realm. I didn't feel much movement in the Word. I wasn't hearing anything from the Lord. My heart seemed to be a bit stuck, not moving in tenderness or any distinguishable breakthrough. A bit discouraged, yet sure of God's desire to be found by me, I kept pacing and praying, praying and pacing, back and forth, over and over, eyes to the ground, as the weeds beneath my feet slowly came into submission, and my path became ever so faintly discernable.

It was on one particular stride down the path when I was suddenly struck by something. There alongside my ever-so-faint footpath were a small group of wildflowers, lifting their heads up to greet me. And then and there I was struck by a possibility. My mind started reasoning. *Why are these flowers here, right alongside this path of mine? Who knows about this path except me...and the Lord? Who is here to enjoy these flowers except me? Has there ever been anyone else back in this overgrown lot except me? Then would it be so far-fetched to assume, that these flowers are in fact planted right here along my path for none other than I?? In all the silence, am I imagining God might have wanted to voice His love to me this day through these flowers, right here along my path? Hmmmm...* And the reasoning went on as my ever-so-small faith sought to sprout from its seed form, fighting against my "better judgment" that I was being childish and seeking to overcome my skepticism that Love could actually be made manifest in such a way.

I'm not sure I fully believed those flowers were for me that day, but something faint changed in me, and my eyes have never been the same. Though I might have begun with mostly skepticism fighting against a tiny bit of faith, as the days went on, the percentages soon changed, and faith and love began to win. Soon I began to see new flowers that were not there the day before, and I was certain of why they were there on these later days. And it wasn't just the flowers. The rain became a signature telling of God's love for me. Every time it rained, no matter what I was doing, I became arrested by God's tender love that He wanted to voice to me. In fact, I was such a believer in this divine-rain-giving that my roommate at the time used to say, "Every time it rains I just think, '*Wow. God sure does love Dana.*'"

In those days one of my big events of the evening was to get in my car right before nightfall and rush up to the top of my favorite hill to watch the sunset. The whole event was all for me. And God's love was so loud through it, so real, so near. I used to watch all of the cars driving on the highway far below and wonder if anyone else in the near vicinity was catching this, if anyone else was claiming what was so readily being offered. And near nightfall, I would watch, as in extreme unnecessary proficiency, God painted the sky with a blaze of color and light, *just for me*. As the heavens declared the glory of God once more in the descending of the sun, I took my place as one receiving this personal expression of God's love—a testimony of His nearness unto me (Ps. 19:1–6).

Recognizing the Unnecessary

Perhaps one of the greatest ways my heart has found to search for His nearness and His reaching out in love unto me is to look around and find some element of His creation, from the sunset to a flower, and say to Him, "That was *unnecessary…*" I look at a sky profuse with colors of every shade, screaming without words of transcendence and Beauty and Love; and I consider how such extravagance didn't *have* to be so. No part of science demanded such magnificence. The sun could have performed its function in light and life without being utterly glorious in its incomings and outgoings. He didn't have to do this. The Creator did not *have* to be so extreme, so radical, and so boundless in His daily creations. All around one looks, to the stars, the sky, the mountains, the oceans, the flowers, and the trees—countless billions of unending beauties lift their voices and all utterly and totally unnecessary, superfluous actions with no technical purpose except the purpose of *love*.

After this recognition of the unnecessary comes the greater leap, the higher conclusion. After aligning my heart with the absolute truth of the unwarranted and excessive nature of these works of God, I go a step further into the leap of faith that says, "And this extravagance is *for me*…this sunset is *for me*…this rain is *for me*…the Lord is *that near* and *that* personal and *that jealous* to win me to Himself in love." There was a day when I thought such reasoning to be childish and egocentric, but I've come to believe the heart that says, "He painted the sky for me," has actually reached a higher height of faith and a greater revelation of the God of love than the heart that concludes nature is the mere meshing of elements and environment—unrelated to the yearnings of the Creator who designed them!

From the beginning of time, even from everlasting, God's love has always been excessive, too much, and extreme.

Shall we believe that He opened the story of Creation with an overabundance of wonder and splendor and then did not proceed to fill each day with that same profusion? And will we limit Him to offering this grand display of all His works on only a *corporate* level, a *general* proclamation and *universal* statement of His love to the world but not a distinctly personal assertion, a deep declaration to each individual heart amidst their unique story and journey? Did He not fashion each one uniquely in the womb, thinking thoughts more numerable than the sand of the seashore as He knit the inmost parts (Ps. 139:13–18)? Could such a One not plan moments of encounter?

It is the personal part that makes all the difference in being changed by such extravagance. If we will allow our eyes to be opened to His persistent love, the love that has been in pursuit of us from everlasting, unyielding and untiring, we will begin to perceive His nearness in every place and to be transformed in a daily way in so doing.

We have considered in this chapter and those preceding it the magnitude of the love of God from all eternity and the extravagance of His self-giving unto us—both in the Gospel and in His daily pursuit of us. Now we turn to that second part of the great exchange—the *response* of our hearts in love unto the God who has given us everything. The Father has willed from eternity to bring us *in* to this same glorious love that He Himself possesses, causing the *very love* with which

He has loved His Son to also be within us—love unspeakably full in its utter givenness (Jn. 17:26). In Part Two, we will delve with greater depth into the theme of how we respond to God's fervent love with great abandonment and extravagance—considering the glories and the difficulties that arise therein. We will take into account the many enemies that would seek to steal our affections and the necessity of warring against them. Finally, we will explore how this love that we give Him is offered both in the ordinary parts of life and in the laying down of our lives in love for one another.

PART TWO:

Our Love

SURRENDERING ENTIRELY

"Jesus said to him, "'You shall love the Lord your God with all your heart, with all your soul, and with all your mind.'"" Matt. 22:37

The Father has willed from eternity to bring us *in* to the same glorious love that He Himself possesses, causing the *very love* with which He has loved His Son to also be within us—love unspeakably *full* in its utter givenness (Jn. 17:26). His overwhelming impartation to us is this burning flame of love—the very ardor eternally alive in Him. And as mysterious as it sounds, though it *is* a mystery surpassing knowledge, this love is not accessed by only the elite few who can attain to it; it is not something only to be known in heightened spiritual encounters or lofty experiences. It is a love given, experienced, and offered in the weakness and commonality of lives such as yours and mine, on days as ordinary as *this one*.

Loving God with all of the heart, soul, mind, and strength can only ever be done in the context of the moments we have been given right now, however ordinary or weak. Yes, we can envision our fervency for God in the future, but it will only remain a dream unless *right now*, in this very moment, we love Him with everything we are, keeping back from Him no conscious area and yielding to Him in every possible way. It is the life of continually communicating with the Holy Spirit in a loving dialogue as we move throughout our day. It means responding to His light when it shines upon our dark places, delighting to give up anything that is revealed as hindering our precious connection and communion to the One that we love—this is loving Him wholly. This utter givenness to Him reflects His own utter givenness to us and in this way we love Him as He has loved us. It is a love not yet of full maturity but of full *measure*, not yet of perfect quality but of *entire quantity*.

Let's consider again what Bernard of Clairvaux so brilliantly stated regarding the subject of our love for God. He said that, though I can never match His love for Me in quantity and quality—if I love Him with all that I am, with my entirety— *"nothing is lacking where everything is given."* When I give Him *everything*—even as He has given everything—this most costly love is the kind for which He seeks. I am not giving Him less than the fullness of what He has requested and desired when I simply give Him all that I am right now, in this season of my life, on this day and not a future day, wholly and without restraint.

Whole Livelihood

The widow who gave her two mites to the treasury exemplifies beautifully this glorious givenness to God. As Jesus sat facing the treasury and watching the people draw near to present their money, He observed many who were rich put in much. Yet what moved His heart more than any other person bringing her offering was this poor widow who submitted only two mites into the treasury. Ten of these mites would have bought a loaf of bread, and a day's wages equaled more than two hundred. Exceptionally small was this offering, yet the heart of love behind it made generous the gift—a treasure of invaluable riches unto Jesus. She gave all that she possessed, her whole livelihood—the greatest gift presented of all (Mk. 12:41–44).

So meager was her offering that it yielded no potential praise of men; in fact, she risked men's *scorn* at bringing so measly a submission. There was no way that she could have done this for the reward of man's approval or for impact—too small was her contribution for these other motives. Thus, we are given insight into the motive Jesus perceived. He recognized the solitary motivation of love for God in this sacrifice.

Compelled by love, this woman did not so despise the smallness of her gift as to withhold it, nor did she refuse to give her offering because it was all that she *had*—her future provision. Against great odds, she gave the smallest gift in terms of tangible amount, yet the greatest in terms of true measure. Moved in His heart, Jesus turned to His disciples and said, "'Assuredly I say to you that this poor widow has put in more than all those who have given to the treasury; for they all put in out of their abundance, but she out of her poverty put in all that she had, her whole livelihood'" (Mk. 12:43–44). She put in *more* because it was entirety enriched with love.

Final Fractions

When Matt said to me that altering statement, "We can be wholehearted right now," I understood to be true both my *current* capacity to give God my all in the present tense, and my *genuine ability* to withhold nothing, my actual *fittedness* to love Him without fractions. Like the widow, I was awakened in a greater way to the truth that I can give Him everything in my life from moment to moment, from thought to thought. In my time, in my speech, in my finances, and in my relationships— on this particular day—I can yield to Him fully and in so doing love Him with a love that comes before the Throne of God as whole and complete.

This is not to say that I can be fully mature in love, *right now*. To be wholehearted does not mean that we've reached the heights of perfection in our devotion unto God. Rather, it means we are *fully given* to Him in every area that we know and perceive, with no conscious place of compromise yet remaining. We are fully yielded to God according to *and in context with* the current revelation that God has given us about our hearts before Him. In every place of our lives, we have responded to His light; in every area, we are deliberately surrendered to Him, embracing His leadership, responding to His illumination, and resisting each enemy of love.

So often we delay in giving God the final fractions of our lives because we want Him to first change our circumstances. We imagine that, when our conditions are different, then finally we will be wholehearted. Yet this is not the order God most often leads us in. He has actually put within our paths each circumstance according to His perfect leadership to create the pressures and difficulties necessary to *produce* a new level of response to Him. We want circumstances to change before we are wholly given, yet God has allowed each circumstance to be part of the plan to actually *bring into being* that full-givenness.

Since the moment of that new understanding, how often I have been going throughout my day, catching myself in a weak spot of heart, thoughts, or words. For example, I will suddenly find my thoughts in one of those imaginary and made-up conversations in which *I* am saying everything right and *I* am the hero of my imagined drama. As I catch myself in such a moment, I realize the fleeting and fleshly nature of these thoughts, and I bring to remembrance the joy God has promised—the joy of fellowship that *could* be mine if only I would surrender that small area and let God take possession of it. I consider what might happen if, rather than spending my thoughts on such transient dramas, I spent them on the beauty of Jesus with a prayer of "I love You, God" in my heart. I think to myself, if I will give this to the Lord and let Him have this area, I could enter into an even *greater* fellowship with His heart. I could be that much closer to Him because of our increased fellowship in the light. Motivated toward that richer communion, that place where the air clears in the distinctive crisp and clean feeling of giving *all* to Him, I yield to the Lord.

Joy in Abandonment

There is an unmistakable and profound joy coming to the heart that withholds nothing from God. Though there is a measure of enjoyment found when we love Him with a good percentage of our lives, He gives to us a pleasure incomparable when we give to Him those final fractions, that last small percentage of *our everything*. It is as though, for the believer, the horizon changes from subtle grays to full color, and the vision is cleared like a fog lifting off of a bright blue sky. There is nothing more exhilarating than the cleanness of living wholly in the light!

This wholehearted givenness to God—a yielding that is rooted and motivated out of *deep love* rather than a duty-based obedience—is truly where all the joy is found! Herein lies the secret of the Kingdom, the treasure of the saint. It is actually the best way to live, the place where finally we are freed from such frantic fighting for ourselves. We at last begin to live in that inexpressible realm of living wholly for God.

When one is wholly given to God—emptied of all, withholding nothing, truly and entirely—then begins the grandness of joy unspeakable, then begins the entrance of eternal pleasures. It is the giving unto God of the final fractions we've gripped so tightly that the fullness of enjoyment is experienced.

We can love God with much of our affections, but if we withhold from Him a portion, we do not enter the extreme pleasures, the untold satisfaction that the whole divine plan intended. And we do not function in the way for which we were designed. It is in the giving of the rest—when at last we yield in every single area from small to great, from subtle to blatant—that the joy of abandonment sets in and the human heart begins to soar regardless of circumstance. Giving God the last portions imparts the brightness of living in the light (Jn. 15:11–13). When this full yieldedness is in place, we are finally free in love, and we become as signposts to the world of something *other-than*, something eternal and beyond, the sure sign of God in our midst (Jn. 13:35).

Such abandonment to God is actually addicting. Those throughout history who have blazed with love for God in the measure that surrenders the final fractions have become obsessed with such loving relinquishing. Their question is not how much God requires of them but rather how much God will allow them to give Him. Rather than clinging to a few last reserves, they are those who search for more to give Him, just so that they might taste of the joy of being fully His, that they might touch the exhilaration of wholeheartedness. This delight is not the religious satisfaction of high performance, which sours our inward parts, nor a perfectionistic drivenness to please, which leaves us feeling condemned. It is experiencing the matchless pleasure of communion with God that we were made for. It is the thrilling exchange of wholly-given love with the One who has wholly given Himself to us.

Entirety Demands Love

The only way to love with this nature of wholeheartedness—this offering of all and withholding of nothing—the only way to actually fulfill the Great Commandment to love God fully is to *fall in love*. Simply put but true nonetheless, we cannot love Him unless we *love* Him, in a very personal way. We cannot climb that great mountain of loving God wholeheartedly unless we ourselves are first *wounded by love*. The command demands a holy lovesickness, and the required prerequisite to fulfill it is a fierce devotion to God. If that *wound* is in place, then when we come against the rigors of this pursuit—when we face the enemies of this abandonment—our wounded hearts of love will leave us no other option, no way of escape, except to embrace Jesus all the more.

Only those who are pierced by the passion of love for Jesus in a personal way eventually will overcome the hindrances of love in heart, soul, mind, and strength. In the great journey of intimacy with God—the epic story of the human heart—the absolutely essential element that must be in place in order to *win* is this *wound of love*, the undeniable affection that wrenches deep and leaves no prisoners.

When one has fallen in love with God, he gets swept away in the jealousy of its nature. It is the *nature* of Love to take over, to conquer all, to overcome every obstacle and be denied at no level. When divine Love is working within the human heart, it begins as a tiny flame and gradually, progressively, becomes a raging, all-consuming fire.

The flaming torches of saints of old from the pages of history, lives lived in loving abandonment unto God, are characterized by this unifying quality—they were wounded by love for God to such a measure that they gave Him everything, in all areas and dimensions. When faced with persecution, mistreatment, and trouble, this flame within shined forth ever brighter, the testimony of love echoing through the generations with the statement of, "He is worthy of everything. There is no cost too high. How infinitely worthy He is of my love."

We have considered the grace that God would give us of full surrender to Himself. This surrender leads us to nothing short of exhilaration in heightened extravagance unto God. There is a place in loving God where we are actually so ruined by the deep workings of passion for Jesus that we are driven to an intense excessiveness in our abandonment to Him. Such forceful love for God has always been provoking by nature and thus often misunderstood and misconstrued by others. Yet this place of great extravagance is an invitation given of God that we do not want to refuse. It is in loving Him extravagantly that we begin to enter a sharing in God's own extravagance—a fellowship in His own extremity of costly love.

CHAPTER 8

*S*ACRIFICING EXTRAVAGANTLY

"If a man would give for love all the wealth of his house, it would be utterly despised." Song of Sol. 8:7

God has opened a wide door to anyone who would desire to love Him in extravagance—anyone who wishes to respond to Him in holy passion. Perhaps one of the greatest examples of all history of one who coursed through that open door without reservation and with unforgettable adoration unto God was Mary of Bethany. Her life modeled this question: "God, just how abandoned will You let me be?"

I've often wondered what happened in the heart of Jesus in the silent moments that followed the breaking open of Mary's alabaster vial and the profusion of fragrant oil that she poured unrestrainedly upon Him. As the moments passed and the tensions and indignation mounted in the room, what was it that arose in the heart of the Son of God? Drenched in fragrance, what struck Him at such a depth and severity that caused Him to finally respond with deep vindication and love (Matt. 26:6–13; Mk. 14:3–9; Jn. 12:1–8).

The anointing took place only days before Jesus' arrest, trial, and crucifixion as He and His disciples gathered for dinner with several friends in the home of Simon the Leper in Bethany. Martha was characteristically serving, and Lazarus, who was just recently raised from the dead, sat reclining at the table with Jesus and all the others (Matt. 26:6; Jn. 12:1–2).

I imagine a sudden bursting open of the door as Mary, younger sister to Martha, entered the room and hurried to the place where Jesus sat. Clenched tightly in her arms was an alabaster box that Martha and Lazarus must have recognized immediately as a family heirloom passed down to Mary. A vial of pure spikenard—the most costly perfume in Palestine, worth more than a full year's wages—was Mary's inheritance, her entire livelihood and provision, kept for her future, now about to be spent in one moment's time.

Without a word from her mouth, yet with a look in her countenance that spoke volumes, she immediately and without hesitation broke the flask and began to pour its contents over the head of Jesus (Matt. 26:7; Mk. 14:3). With a gasp of shock, the room fell into a tense silence, a hushed atmosphere thick with allegation and yet *permeated* in fragrance (Matt. 26:8–9; Mk. 14:4; Jn. 12:5).

Waste or Wisdom?

In these moments, the One whose name is the Word of God sat silent without a word given until after the disciples challenged Mary's offering (Mk. 14:6; Jn. 12:7). I believe in these moments of delay—as the profuse fragrance drenched His head and feet, filling every sense with its aroma— something profoundly tremendous transpired in the heart of Jesus. Here He was, days before His crucifixion and heavy with the weighty events just before Him. Many times had He spoken of these impending tragic events to His disciples, yet they still were predominantly disconnected from what so ominously lie ahead. Yet this young woman, the one who also sat at His feet with a hungry heart to hear His words, had *heard* with her heart the predictions Jesus made of His coming death, and she came now with a response rooted in love (Lk. 10:39). She knew His hour was at hand. He was about to give all, and she wanted to do the same. She desired to give Him an offering before that day, an anointing of His body for His burial, a drenching of love and honor worthy of this true King. Having "kept" this oil for this day, we know this act was wrought in premeditated moments of love and holy devotion, a conscious and planned choosing in her heart to pour out her *entire inheritance* over Him before He died (Jn. 12:7).

As the bottle was broken, the oil emptied upon Jesus, and the fragrance wafted generously through the room, the pulsating silence was seared by severe charges of the indignant disciples. "Why this waste?!" went forth their accusation, "This perfume could have been sold and given to the poor!" With voices sharp and cruel, they criticized Mary for her foolishness, calling it waste, excessive, and pointless loss (Matt. 26:8; Mk. 14:4–5; Jn. 12:5). Somehow this impassioned act of voluntary love instantaneously exposed a definite dullness in the hearts of these men. Their indignation blinded their hearts enough to believe this anointing of the King to be excessive and unnecessary, wasteful and foolish.

Silencing the disciples' criticism with a clear vindication, Jesus spoke, "'Let her alone; she has kept this for the day of My burial. For the poor you have with you always, but Me you do not have always'" (Jn. 12:7–8). To this statement of Jesus, Mark's gospel adds, "'She has done a good work for Me…wherever this gospel is preached…what this woman has done will be told as a memorial to her'" (Mk. 14:6–9).

Jesus received this act of devotion as something eternally precious to His heart, an identification with His suffering to come and a connection with the impending crucifixion only days away. The disciples looked at the extravagance and called it unnecessary waste, yet *Jesus* received it as something exceedingly treasured, to be remembered as a memorial and preached always wherever His Gospel would be proclaimed.

I believe that as Jesus looked into the heart of this young woman and perceived her intense resolve of love and sacrifice, He recognized an eternal attribute of *His own* love—a love that gives entirely. Mary's voluntary sacrifice to give Jesus her security for the future resounded with the characteristic of love reminiscent of His own sacrifice—the love that gives everything and withholds nothing. Jesus saw this absoluteness in her offering, this perfection of surrender, and His heart was moved beyond measure.

Unnecessary Love

Mary was not doing what was required of her; she was doing the *unnecessary*, and this was the beauty of her offering. When the disciples called her offering *waste*, they were *right* in the sense that she did not *have* to give so extravagantly. She could have loved Jesus and honored Him without pouring over Him her full inheritance, her certainty of the future, her stability for tomorrow. And yet, it was in this very voluntary aspect that I believe Jesus' heart was so greatly moved. She did not *have* to, and yet she *did*. She volunteered her love freely even as Jesus volunteered His love freely from everlasting. She gave excessively even as He has always given excessively, unnecessarily, and without reserve.

God has eternally "wasted" profusely in His love and in His sacrifice, and this is the very nature of His love. God could have redeemed us and kept us at a distance forever and still remained "good" for all eternity. Yet He went so *far* in His extravagance. In our book, He broke every rule in His unthinkable abundance, crossing every line in His sheer excessiveness. He gave with a sacrificial rending that will thunder for thousands upon thousands of years into and throughout the ages.

His extravagant offerings are not limited to the incarnation and crucifixion but given each day in every beauty found in nature, in every goodness we experience in relationships, even in every moment of time and every breath of life that we breathe. As James states, "Every good gift and perfect gift is from above and comes down from the Father of lights, with whom there is no variation or shadow of turning" (James 1:17). His is a love that volunteers itself with sacred excess and holy, unnecessary abundance.

I believe it was this same sort of profusion that Jesus beheld in Mary's offering. I believe He recognized the holy eternal devotion that burned in His own heart. He saw within her the godly affection that withholds nothing, and her devotion greatly moved Him. It is what He's looking for in all the earth as His eyes search to and fro: voluntary lovers who will love Him in extravagance even as He has loved lavishly from all eternity.

The Good News

When Jesus said, "'Wherever this gospel is preached in the whole world, what this woman has done will also be told as a memorial to her,'" He voiced His command that this portrait be included in the telling of the true Gospel (Matt. 26:13). I believe that, in this decree, He deemed this extravagant act of devotion as a necessary illustration of what the good news of the Gospel is all about—radical and unreserved love, first from the heart of God unto us and then returned from our hearts unto Him.

The great story of the eternal ages is about the *unnecessary, wasteful, excessive* offering of love. With this love God has loved us, and with this same kind of love He wants to be loved. The good news of all time is far beyond the legal position we have been offered in Christ. The entrance we have been given and the access we have been allowed are unthinkable, unspeakable—of such proximity to leave us struck and stunned in gratitude for all eternity. We will fall on our faces in worship again and again and again, ten thousand times ten thousand, never wearying in wonder and love at the grandeur of what we have been given and the profusion of extremity in God's love for us.

Personally Responding in Love

Mary of Bethany responded to God in extravagance, giving Him her everything, because she was moved by love. And the way she was moved by love is that she took deeply personal the love of Christ. She heard His words not just as one among many but as though He were speaking directly to her. She remembered His prediction of His coming death and was moved to respond in a very personal way. She took no thought of how the others responded or what they did or didn't do. He had spoken His heart to *her*, and she responded to Him in love.

Jesus looked at the costly offering that Mary poured upon Him and spoke a phrase so remarkable, "'She has done what she could'" (Mk. 14:8). He considered His coming cross, His desire for friendship and fellowship in the hour of His suffering, and He said in essence, "Mary has done her part. She has responded in love with all her heart, and I receive it. She has fulfilled her role in this great Story, and I will remember it forever" (Mk. 14:9).

The gifts that we give God are put within our hands by Him. We cannot give Him anything except what He has first given us. We cannot love Him except with the love that He first loved us with (1 Jn. 4:19). From before her creation, it was determined that this gift would be placed within Mary's hands and she would have the choice in voluntary love to pour it out upon Jesus before His death. Each of us has access to a wholehearted surrendering, a gift given of God that is in our reach to bestow upon Him. He does not demand nor force it in such a way as to remove the voluntary aspect. He waits for us to *want* to give it to Him. When we lift this gift, this offering of our *all* back to the Lord, we add our part to the great Story of love being written.

Oh, that Jesus would look at our lives and say this phrase that crowned Mary's life, "She has done what she could," or "He has done what he could." Oh, that we would receive His love and His words in such a personal way that we would be moved with the same abandonment, compelled to love Him so extravagantly.

Loving God in the way He is worthy to be loved, as we have seen, will cost us everything. Such extravagance of living not only comes at a high price but with a constant fight. Such a potency of passion does not stay fueled automatically, and in our fallenness, our propensity is continually towards dullness rather than fiery love. It's toward partiality rather than whole givenness. Over and over again, we have looked at the feasibility of loving God *wholly* from moment to moment. Along with this possibility comes the parallel necessity of continually resisting every enemy of love—constantly fleeing the darkness and dullness that would so subtly destroy the simplicity of our devotion unto God (2 Cor. 11:3).

CHAPTER 9

REFUSING PARTIALITY

"Do not love the world or the things in the world. If anyone loves the world, the love of the Father is not in him." 1 Jn. 2:15

Perhaps one of the greatest surprises and perplexities to me as I have journeyed with the Lord—seeking to love Him with all that I am, heart, soul, mind, and strength—is how *quickly* I lose the strength of my devotion by the subtle destroyers of dullness. I have been surprised by how *often* it is necessary to sign up all over again, to reconnect with the vision of abandonment, and to reengage in battle against the enemies that would seek to destroy my love for Him. I find myself in need of constant realignment with the very things that burned within me just a few days prior. It truly requires desperation to love God with everything, and such desperation cannot stay fervent and alive without relentless cultivation and replenishing.

To love Him with all my heart is something I do and something I offer to Him not "once and for all" but a thousand times a thousand, day after day after day. Countless foes of every kind resist such an offering and hinder such an emptying at every turn. The most powerful thing in the world is a heart overcome by love, and thus the enemies of such a reality are fierce and constant. In one day's time, I can begin to grow subtly distant, subtly cold, subtly guarded within. Without even realizing it, the weeds of doubt can creep up among the tender soils of my soul and strangle the small fragrant flowers of love's cultivation within me. And thus, while my lips continue to speak the same words—words of desperation and longing and desire—my heart may all the while be bearing up walls, forging defenses, and harboring hesitations. While my mouth may be full of grandiose statements concerning how wholly I do love Him, and my words abundant in extravagant requests for His coming to me, my heart might be filled with subtle defenses, walled up and reticent, on its way to becoming stiff and hard and obstinate.

How great are the opposers of loving God vehemently. The enemies of love are many, and Satan's greatest strike is at the simplicity of devotion that we began the journey with (2 Cor. 11:3). Yet this is not cause for lost hope. For as strong as the enemy and fierce the foes of wholeheartedness before God, ten thousand times greater is His own jealousy, His own power to protect and overcome every opponent if only I continually respond to His leading and His love. I cannot keep my own heart, yet the Jealousy that formed the worlds surrounds me as a fortress on every side.

Jesus is deeply acquainted with my weakness, my propensity to lose my focus, and my inability to sustain the fire of my own heart, and yet none of these limitations are troublesome to Him. His confidence to bring me into the perfection of love is in *His own strength* and not mine. What He wants from me and is looking to find is a heart that *keeps responding* to Him, keeps crying out for and receiving His help all along the way to overcome the obstacles and triumph over the enemies. He is not looking for a love devoid of all weakness but a love that adamantly cleaves to His own divine might over and over again. He wants me to live refusing that my love for Him be diffused or dulled, that I may continually be ready to do whatever is necessary to remain vibrant and alive, with devotion ever deepening rather than growing cold as the years elapse. This is how love wins over its enemies—first by God's own relentless jealousy and power and second by my continuous, full response to Him. This response entails my persistent cry for His help and my refusal to live in less than the progressive perfecting of love in my life.

God has given us many pictures in creation to depict the spiritual principle that love must be persistently cultivated if it is to excel. One of the most repeated pictures is that of a garden, symbolizing our inner life in God (Song of Sol. 4:12;

Mk. 4:3-20). It is very natural for weeds, temptations, to spring up repeatedly in a garden with healthy soil. To struggle with weeds is not wickedness, but letting them grow unchecked is. The only way to have a weed-free garden is by actually pulling the weeds day after day. This involves considerable labor, but the rewards of enjoying unhindered love and fruitfulness far outweigh the effort. "Above all else," says Wisdom, "guard your heart, for it is the wellspring of life" (Prov. 4:23).

The Vow Amidst Weakness

As I have found this continual need to reconnect with my vision and regularly stir myself to return to the "first works" of my first love, I have often felt great disillusionment as to how I could lose my way so quickly (Rev. 2:5). Yet in this disillusionment, the Lord has revealed again and again that what is a surprise to me is *not* a surprise to Him. He knows the frailty of the human heart, and when we say "yes" to Him, with all our fervor, He knows that there are "holes" riddled throughout our vow. And yet, though we have weakness in our commitment to Him, He does not despise or reject our declaration and our heart intention. Rather, He receives it as *exactly* what He is looking for and desires. He knows that we cannot fulfill it without His power and perfect leadership, and He knows that in only a matter of days we will grow distant and dulled from it, needing a new resolve once again. Yet still He does not despise it but receives it as *real love* for Him.

We cannot say "yes" to the high vision one day and have that single vow hold us through until the final day. Far from that, our vows to the Lord are something given and something offered over and over, every few days, realigning our hearts, resisting dullness and re-signing up once more. This is actually how it looks to move forward in love. Who would have thought that love would look so weak? Yet God knew it all along. He is not looking for perfect track records but for a continual receiving of His heart and His strength day by day as we progress along our way in love.

This process of growing in love is weak the whole way in the sense that those most mature are those most dependent upon the Lord. In this life, we never graduate from our weakness, and yet in another sense we get stronger and stronger because our love for God and our gratitude in His kindness to us grow increasingly.

As we grow in dependence upon God, knowing our weakness and yet receiving His strength, our love and gratitude unto God grows and expands. As our experience of His love amidst our weakness increases, we become ruined for any lesser thing and increasingly willing to forsake all things that keep us in any way hindered from knowing and experiencing His heart. And this is the progression of how God perfects love in us. He first "ruins" us by His love and then in the midst of that ruined state, He invites us to yield ourselves to Him in every way.

Chapter 9

God the Jealous Husband

God is a jealous Lover, fierce in His extremity, whole-hearted in His refusal to be denied. He has called Himself the All Consuming Fire and the Jealous God. He is unchanging in this nature. He wants all of us in every measure, desiring to overcome within us every small area of compromise, sin, and darkness. When we say "yes" to Him, *He says "yes"* to our willing heart and begins the great take-over of every intricate part of us. Like a conquering king of the ancient day, He begins the gradual subduing of every part of us, yet with an incessant dedication to never violate our free will, refusing to move forward in this conquering at any level unless we are fully and completely *willing* and *wanting* His holy advancement in our lives.

We see this aspect of the heart of God greatly portrayed in the Song of Solomon journey, when Jesus comes to the young Bride as One leaping upon the mountains, powerfully conquering all the opponents of love (Song of Sol. 2:8–10). With zeal and abandon, He invites her to arise to the mountains *with Him*, to leave behind the fears and small compromises that subtly hinder and destroy her love.

Up until this point in the Song, Jesus' main objective in leading the Bride forward in love is to convince her of His unyielding and unrelenting affection for her. He has showered her with abundance of fellowship and love. In absolute joy, the Bride has responded to His love, saying of Him that His love is far superior to any lesser pleasures in all the created order. She drinks deeply of His affection and becomes ruined by it, wounded by it, stating that she is absolutely lovesick and in need of more and more of God (Song of Sol. 1:2–2:4).

At the timing of this invitation, we find the Bride in a place of drinking deeply of these superior pleasures of God, fully content to remain in this posture as she enjoys the Lord's presence and basks in the wonderful experience of His love. Still in spiritual infancy, she has no idea the Lord is about to come and disrupt her spiritual haven out of His fierce commitment to His radical intention to bring her into spiritual maturity and ultimately true partnership with Himself.

From Sincerity to Entirety

This scene in the Song of Solomon storyline portrays a great crossroads on the expedition of loving God. It is the point on love's journey where *sincerity* must meet *severity* and be converted into *entirety*. This is where the Lord brings each one of us as we move forward with Him in holy devotion. He is on the mission of the great "take-over" of the whole of our lives. He wills to gradually and progressively convert our initial *sincerity* into an eventual *entirety*, overcoming every enemy that keeps us bound, and subduing every compromise and fear that holds us back.

Jesus wants all of us and not just a part. He is jealous that we would not remain in the place of immaturity, though our hearts are sincere, but move into the fullness of love, where our love is entire. The nature of Love is to capture all, to consume everything. A husband that truly loves his wife could never say to her, "I have reached the point where my love for you stops. I'll love you this much, but not more." Love is not love if it remains stagnant—it must keep conquering until it has won altogether. The love of God possesses a jealousy that is as cruel as the grave—with a grasp as comprehensive as death holds over the natural. It is a most vehement flame that consumes all and is not extinguished even by many waters or floods (Song of Sol. 8:6).

The Wound of Love

In order for love to win—we must respond wholly at every point to this Jealous Husband. Our desperation must increasingly mount up, and our wound of love in our hearts must steadily deepen so that, when He comes with an invitation to arise, we might be so *ruined*, so overcome, with so many bridges burned behind us, that we want no other alternative. We must embrace Him wholly.

This ruined state that we find ourselves in is where the wound of love becomes as a friend our hearts desire, and even need, to help us respond to God in desperation. We have looked at how *entirety demands love,* and here is one of the most vivid applications of that need. When Jesus comes to us with an invitation to leave our areas of compromise, whether in thought or word or deed, we could try to conjure up the will to obey Him a thousand times, attempting to fight our way through these barricades and in our own effort force ourselves into fullness. Yet all of this straining will never get the job done. The only way to give Him all that He asks is to be gripped by love for this One who Himself gave all, to be undone and overcome in affection for He who withheld *nothing*—to so greatly suffer the infliction of Love's invasion upon the heart to such a degree that I have no desire to turn Him away. Bound by a lovesick heart, I receive Him at every point.

In order to give God our everything, surrendering to Him in every area from small to great, we need to be wounded with what saints in history called the "incurable wound." We need our hearts to be moved in a deeply personal way by the Person of Christ, filled with undying passion. It is this passion—this delightful and incurable wound—that will contribute most to the great conversion of our souls.

Rather than looking for a way of escape from His incessant invitation, when my heart has undergone the wounding of love, I become desperate to find another bridge to burn, another compromise to flee, another fear to forsake, so that Jesus might enjoy even more of His inheritance in me, and so that I might live and taste even more freely of that glorious realm of being wholly His. It is this wounding of love—imposed upon my heart by the One who *is* Love—that will ultimately make possible so great a surrender.

At the end of the story, Love will triumph over all. The Love of perfection will *remain* while all that is in part will be done away (1 Cor. 13:8–10). What began from eternity past in Trinitarian Love, in that far-reaching realm that we can only form so faint of a conception, will culminate in a triumphant take-over, a winning victory as God's relentless love is returned from His people with an unrelenting, abandoned response.

Throughout our reflection of what it is to love God with our all, we have taken into account that such a love is comprised of the ordinary moments of our day-to-day lives. Now let us look into this concept with greater detail, asking the Lord to change our paradigm of loving God from being a distant and future wholeheartedness to a *present* and *current* abandonment.

CHAPTER 10

OFFERING THE ORDINARY

"For this commandment which I command you today is not too mysterious for you, nor is it far off...the word is very near you, in your mouth and in your heart, that you may do it."' Deut. 30:11, 14

In all of my doings, all of my comings and goings, so much of what I have to offer to the Lord is that which begins as common, that which is mundane and ordinary. If I wait to offer Him only something "spiritual," only that which seems sacred, I will have a small offering, if any. Life is made up of thousands of ordinary moments on ordinary days as we do common tasks for common people and fulfill everyday assignments throughout our everyday lives.

We only have these days, given of God, filled with all of their ordinary contents, in which to love the Lord and find fellowship with Him. The future that we think of so often may or may not happen—we cannot be certain. We cannot plan with sureness on what we will do tomorrow, always planning as if we could guarantee that we even *have* tomorrow (James 4:13–15). We have but *one window* that we are sure of in which we might offer the Lord the whole of our hearts—all that we are—and that window is *now*. The problem with right now is that it seems so ordinary, so non-mysterious, and so common-place. How could it be that *this* is the context in which the Lord would want to commune with me, find fellowship, and reveal love? And yet it is, without question.

When God first proclaimed the first commandment, inviting His people to love Him wholly, He affirmed the truth that this command, this way of living, is not too far off in the distance for each one to live it out in his own context. He assured it is not so grandiose that the lowly could not attain to it, nor is it too lofty or mysterious that the simple heart would be kept from it (Deut. 30:11, 14). It is near us, in our mouths and in our hearts.

The simplicity of this command is actually that which would keep us most distant from it, assuming we do not know how to love Him or we cannot love Him in the way He would want us to. Yet the context where love is cultivated and exchanged truly happens in the common. The atmosphere in which the first commandment is fulfilled is in the simplicity and consistency of devotion unto Him in the day-to-day, moment-to-moment basics of life (2 Cor. 11:3). Here and no other place is where we love God fully.

The Common Made Sacred

Commonness is the nature of human life in the age of time. It is the only sort of context we are given to love God within. According to the divine brilliance of everlasting wisdom, this is the environment in which love for God and man is cultivated, maintained, and offered.

When the light of this truth went on in my understanding, I began to see each ordinary moment as a possible exchange with Jesus. Hundreds of times I have been in the middle of my average moments, fixing lunch or singing to my little girl, driving in my car or just getting ready in the morning, and I will remember, by the whispering of the Holy Spirit, I can be wholehearted *right now*. These common moments could be sacred if I would live them with an "I love You" in my heart. The Lord continues to reveal to me that these seemingly static seconds of time have hidden doorways in them if I will choose to seek out their invitation. The secret of the many saints of history, the heroes of the faith, is not that they managed to do only "spiritual" things, but that they learned how to make *common* things *sacred* unto the Lord. They learned that God can be loved continually and can be known always, not just in times set apart for prayer or in lofty spiritual experiences, but in the commonness of life, the everyday moments and even the busy comings and goings. If we do not find Him *there*, in the ordinary tasks and circumstances, we will not somehow suddenly find Him in times defined as "sacred."

Chapter 10

The well-known Brother Lawrence, the man famous for doing the service of kitchen work and cobbling shoes with the utmost love for God and continual communion with Him, lived a life that captured this truth beautifully and profoundly. His life has become as a shining example, both in word and in works, of what it looks like to love God with everything, even amidst the commonness of everyday life. It was said of Brother Lawrence:

> *He found no more excellent means of going to God than the ordinary actions which were prescribed to him through obedience, purifying them as much as he was able of every human aspect, and doing them solely for the love of God. It is a grave error to believe that fixed prayer times are different from any other time, for we are as strictly obliged to be united to God through our duties in their appropriate time as by prayer in its time…When the appointed times of prayer were past, he found no difference, because he still continued with God, praising and blessing Him with all his might…* *

Brother Lawrence understood the simplicity of loving God in all things, with no separations between that which was spiritual and that which was common, but with a continual offering unto God in love every part of his day, every word from his mouth, every small and tiny task. With a simple

---

* Brother Lawrence, *The Practice of the Presence of God*, p. 75–76 (Paraclete Press, 1985).

wisdom that rings with the sound of Jesus' Gospel given unto the meek and lowly, he spoke:

> *We must trust God once and for all and abandon our-*
> *selves to Him alone. He will not deceive us. We must*
> *not grow weary of doing little things for the love of God,*
> *who looks not on the great size of the work, but on the*
> *love in it.**

Jesus Crowned the Common

The greatest testament of the *nobility* of loving God amidst the smallest parts of common life is found in the life of Jesus. We are given the highest exemplification of the dignity of serving in the "unimportant" and unrecognized by watching Him embrace commonness in the incarnation and observing how He did not despise the simple things in His earthly life. He joyed in the everyday duties and tasks and did not see them as unfitting or too trivial to love His Father amidst.

Jesus knew a secret that He wanted to reveal to us through the demonstration of His life. The secret was the Father actually *rewards* faithfulness in the mundane (Mk. 9:41). The assignments and job descriptions He gives us often seem so small that we would be prone to despise them. Yet herein is where He is looking for faithfulness and love (Matt. 25:23; Lk. 16:10; 19:17). And this is the secret Jesus wanted us to know.

---

* ibid.

Chapter 10

Growing up as the son of a carpenter, Jesus became a carpenter Himself and spent the *thirty years* before His earthly ministry in near total obscurity, doing the ordinary parts of life like all those surrounding Him, never deeming it too insignificant or too minor (Mk. 6:3). During this time, He did not preach or do miracles; He did not gather crowds or make a name for Himself. So obscure was His life for this thirty-year span that, from the time Jesus was twelve in the temple to when His ministry finally emerged, we have little recorded mention of its detail.

Jesus knew human experience. He knew monotony. He knew the day to day. He was acquainted with the common and not a stranger to the trivial. Truly, in all ways, He is our Brother. When we are cleaning our houses, mowing our lawns, playing with our children, driving in our cars, He is deeply and intimately near and familiar—inviting us to follow His example in loving God extravagantly amidst our present obscurity.

By Jesus' embracing of the human plight, He made way for each moment of monotony to be a doorway of fellowship. There is nothing too small, no circumstance too trivial that we cannot bring to Him in love, having conversation with Him in the midst of it and consecrating it unto Him as something done in love. He reaches to us in our boredom, in our ordinary and routine aspects of life, and invites us to love Him in all parts of our day, all through the ordinary activities and obscure tasks of necessity. If we seek for Him here, He is present to be found by us. And as we are faithful to offer Him these things, doing everything as unto the Lord, even the smallest cup of cold water given will have eternal reward (Mk 9:41).

Giving God Everything

It is as though our Beloved Jesus would say to us: "If you love Me, truly love Me, then give Me everything. To keep My commands, to keep My word is not mysterious, and it is not a cold and stiff sort of living but a living near at hand, a living saturated and immersed in love. Keeping My commands means offering Me everything in love in all the parts of life, all the parts of the day, all the ordinary, and all the mundane. Love is displayed and made manifest in the open theater of the everydayness of life. From this stage and no other you exhibit your affections for Me. I do not wait for any other song and dance, any other presentation than this. If you do not give me the everydayness, you will never love Me with the extraordinary. If you do not offer Me the small, you will not offer Me the big. If you do not make the common an offering, you will never be equipped within to give Me the so-called 'spiritual.'"

Jesus did not say to us that the one who loves Him is the one who tells Him often or makes confessions sublime. It is not only by our many expressions that we convey our love to Him, not just through our spiritual declarations, but in deed and in truth (1 Jn. 3:18). Our love for Him also goes far beyond those actions that we would define as *sacred* and can be observed in the simplest deeds of careful obedience to His word in every moment.

Anyone who has learned the secret of such moment-to-moment obedience knows that the strength behind the surrender, the power compelling the offering, is the *movement of love* and the heart of a lover. When someone lives out obedience to God's Word in the ordinary parts of life, in the unperceived and overlooked hiddenness of the mundane, we can be sure that something great has happened deep inside his heart. This practical obedience is actually the open display of a love that has conquered the most hidden parts of the heart. It is the outward manifestation of the inward cultivation, the external exhibit of the internal flame.

Martyrdom begins in the Mundane

I've heard it said that in one sense it is easier to be a martyr than to die daily for the cause of love. The reason is that martyrdom happens in only a few minutes while dying daily—laying down our lives in the midst of ordinary circumstance and run-of-the-mill relationship dynamics—takes far more effort and far more givenness while producing far less appreciation from those around us and rendering no accolade or applause from men. While our earthly lives *might* include one or two climactic events—such as in the beauty of martyrdom for Christ, in which our passion and devotion for God is displayed in extravagant sacrifice before the eyes of *many*—

these rare pinnacle moments are truly the exception as compared to the thousands of hidden forms of extravagance we offer in love before the eyes of *One* in the day to day.

God has designed this pilgrimage of life to be comprised in the majority of mundane circumstance and obscure living. The only way we will *eventually* love God fully, in culmination moments such as persecution or suffering for Christ, is if we *presently* love God fully in the commonplace and everydayness of our lives. Only if we daily give our lives, a continual dying to ourselves, will we ever be prepared in heart and life to one day give our lives, even unto death, if the Lord does so invite us.

In our desire to be wholehearted, our craving to be abandoned and not mediocre in love, we have to know that the only way forward is to live fully in love and fully alive in the midst of the mundane. These ordinary moments are not to be despised but embraced. They are not foreign to Jesus, and He does not despise them as we so often do. He is looking for love in them, seeking exchange amidst them, and inviting us to true fellowship with Himself through them.

What began as a notion that loving God wholly was *too mysterious* is now before us like a constant open door, so blatantly accessible in the commonplace that we could never write it off as too difficult to attain to. And herein we find that God has *yet another* surprise for us in this opened invitation. The ordinary moments present to us opportunities for encounter with God—indeed the very context for love to grow.

Additionally, our *relationships* with others—our interactions with every person from spouse to friend, to enemy—make available to us the highest dimensions and greatest expressions of loving God with all that we are. Where we have sought to love Him from a distance, we are confronted with the pressing proximity of opportunity for love to grow and abound through the offering of our lives unto those around us. And this is exactly what He intended to happen. When He asked us to love Him as He has loved us, He brought us into the full circle that culminates in loving others as we love ourselves (Matt. 22:39).

CHAPTER 11

OVERFLOWING OUTWARDLY

"'Love one another; as I have loved you.'" Jn. 13:34

In all my years of loving God—pursuing the fullness
of intimacy with Him, desiring to encounter Him and be
encountered by Him—a most unexpected surprise has crept
up on me in the unlikely occasions prevalently supplied in *being
a mom.* Of all of my responsibilities in life thus far, perhaps
nothing has caused a greater holy fear in me than the trembling task of bringing forth little hearts and seeking to lead in
love these ones whose spirits are eternal. I have found that as
I've entered this weighty role of responsibility, my desperation
for continual "help" from the Lord has intensified greatly. And
with this increased sense of inadequacy, so too has grown my
sense of His presence and my continual loving converse with
Him. Never have I been so in need, so connected to my

inability, and so desperate for His leadership. This great need has been an unexpected escort for me into a sort of ongoing communion with God that I have for years asked the Lord for.

The Great Sanctifier

As a new mom, I have just crossed the threshold into the room I've heard called, "the great sanctifier," and found within these chambers a hundred daily opportunities to desperately draw upon the great Vine in whom I abide and thirstingly drink of that great Source who finds His abode in me. The nature of a sanctifier is it provides an avenue of purifying for the places that all other means cannot get to, the unseen parts that do not get touched through other measures. With two children under the age of three, I have only begun this purification process, yet so soon am I benefiting from its workings. Daily I find things operating in my heart and arising out of me that grieve the Lord and have potential to mark my children wrongly…and this is the pain that leads me to the place of dire need.

Desperation born out of true inability and weakness has been as my escort to rush me to the end of myself and there connect me more deeply to Life Himself. With every word born in frustration, every response rising from pride, every hasty act emerging out of irritation, a searing sobriety confronts me. By the force of Love, I am instantly connected to my poverty of spirit and driven desperately to God.

And herein is the surprise. Found within that mysterious truth that "I can do nothing apart from Him," I find His Presence so real in the midst of my *need*. As I draw near to Jesus in my reach of powerlessness, I am experiencing a profound return of *His* reach toward me. It is as though in that true cry for help and true recognition of poorness, His heart is arrested and He cannot resist answering. Perfecting His strength in my weakness, He rushes in with the help that I need and the Presence that brings my heart right back into remembrance of the Love that is my only Source. My need is truly my escort.

Again and again, I am finding that, when yielded to, this River called Love overcomes my foes of pride, frustration, and impatience. As I reach for God from the place of my weakness and need, Love again takes me into its rolling billows, taking me deeper into the fellowship for which I was made.

This communion is actually *catching*. As I draw upon that Vine in the hundred small circumstances of common parenting or common services throughout my day, I am beginning to find Him more deeply and more sweetly in all the dimensions of life. Returning to my chair for a few sacred moments of prayer during the hush of naptime, this communion begun in the common tensions and ordinary activities continues in my "set apart" time of prayer, even enhancing the exchange.

Chapter 11

Encountering Jesus in Low Places

What a surprise it is to find that our own weakness amidst loving and serving others—our own leaning and limping in our relationships—can become for us the avenue by which we find the One our hearts have longed for, searched and pined after. He is so often not where we thought we would find Him. And yet, this should be no surprise when we consider who it is for whom we search. The One that we love is the One who has bowed lower than any Man. He is the meekest and the lowliest—the most humble of all—and His greatest pursuit is the hearts of weak and broken people. How often we search for Him in all the "high places" only to come across Him in the most common and simple, even the most weak and broken situations. He is the Man who was rich yet became poor, the One who did not despise the lowest place, plunging Himself lower than conceivably possible, further down than any sense of "dignity" would allow for, lower and lower still.

Thus, it is—as we lower ourselves in love and sacrifice to another, choosing the road of meekness, embracing the place of surrender—the surprise awaiting us is our Jesus, low and behold, in that lowest place of self-emptying. As we empty ourselves and get beneath others in order to lift them higher, there below us is Jesus, always beneath, always meek, always emptying Himself in love, and continually using His strength to lift up and empower the weak ones. In our own self-lowering, offered in love unto God, we find Him there, pouring out His love toward us, desirous to strengthen our love at every turn, and filling us with renewed communion with Himself. It is these low and least expected places that often yield the most sweet and greatest fellowship.

Converging of Two Great Commands

I am beginning to see more clearly that great relationship between the first and second command of God, that great mystery of overlap and intersection between the two. Loving others is the grand theater of *real life drama* where our love for God is enacted and played out; hence, the Lord referred to this second commandment as like the first (Matt. 22:39). This continuity and likeness between the two commands is evidenced in that my love for God is strengthened and intensified as I pour out my life unto another. Love begets love and as I give of myself to others, the certain outcome is a greater and deeper love for God and an expanded experience of His own love for me. In the same way, as I give myself wholly unto God, my love for another is enriched beyond measure.

When we lay down our lives, from small ways to substantial, we are pouring out our offering of love unto God, loving Him by loving another, turning every act of service— every dying to self, every lowering of ourselves for the lifting of another—into an act of love. If we truly love Him, this is the way that we continually demonstrate our love (1 Jn. 4:21).

When we love another, we love Him, and in loving Him we lay down our lives for one another.

The nature of love once more is seen in the whole-hearted giving of itself, and this too is where the two commands overlap and intersect. Whether we love God or we love our neighbor, the focus is upon *the laying down of our own lives* in fullness. The overlap is found in the entire self-emptying required for the fulfillment of both charges.

Freedom of Love

As we yield in faithfulness to a *full abandonment* to love, whether that love be directed to God or man or both, the *ease* of love sets in—the commands become no longer burdensome (1 Jn. 5:3). In the dying to myself—the laying down of my rights, my desires, my wants, and the offering of my life to another—a certain freedom enters that was never there before.

Once again, we were made to be abandoned, and we were made to live, *truly live*, in the context of genuinely giving ourselves on behalf of another. It isn't just that these commands are the highest because they are the most noble or righteous. They are the highest way to live because only in living them do we enter that brilliant state of abandon for which we were created. They are the greatest because they ask for the entirety we were made for. They are comprehensive. They sum up the Law and the Prophets—all the revelations of what God desires and requires (Mt. 22:40).

We were made to live with hearts bursting in love and soaring in freedom. That life is ascertained and that freedom is found only when we cease the frenzied fight of self-promotion, self-absorption, and self-gain. Abiding in such self-centeredness is for the soul a remaining in death, but in the loving of our brothers, we pass from death to life (1 Jn. 3:14). When we take the leap of laying our lives down, daring to forget ourselves on behalf of another, and venturing out of the suffocation of self-regard, *fresh Life* floods our souls.

The one in love is the one truly free, and thus it is the lover who cannot be controlled or bound by externals. Nothing can be taken from them outwardly because inwardly they have already given everything. And who can steal from one who has given all? Saint John Chrysostom stated beautifully:

> *"Tell me, what are we afraid of? Death? Christ is my life, and death is my victory. Exile? The earth is the Lord's and the fullness thereof. The loss of earthly goods? We brought nothing into this world, and certainly we can carry nothing out of it. As for the dangers of the world, I despise them, and as for its magnificence, I scorn it. I do not fear poverty, and have no need of riches; I am not afraid of death, I do not wish to live, unless it is for your good. That is why I am exhorting you today to take comfort..."*[*]

---

[*] Aime Puech, *St. John Chrysostom*, p. 162 (Benziger, 1902).

Chapter 11

Two Commands: One River

The indwelling Holy Spirit, who pours out the love of God within our hearts, does not reach from two different sources in which to issue forth love (Rom. 5:5). Rather, when *love for God* or *love for others* is alive within our hearts, *one single* operation of the Holy Spirit is presently at work. We would often like to separate our love for God from our love for others, finding comfort in our seeming abandonment to God while our love for others might be on the neglected side. Yet these divisions are not accurate measurements. Again, we do not draw from *one* river's source to love God and *another* to love people. It is all the same River as it is all the same Source (Rom. 5:5).

My love for God is no higher and no greater than the love displayed in the weak, and at-times, tense moments of relating to those I love. These *windows of weakness* are revealers of the degree in which love has truly conquered and taken leadership in my life. I cannot hang curtains over them and then go sit alone in my room with God and imagine myself to love Him greatly. Rather, I must peer through them and allow them to be my revealers into the furtherance of love's conquering in my life. At each hasty word—each swelling of frustration—the window opens, and the test of love begins.

When in the frictions of these times of tension, I reach out of my poverty for that Love that is greater than all of my lovelessness, the God of Love hears and answers. He responds with every grace needed to lay down my life even as He laid down His, and in this exchange, Love overcomes; Love wins (1 Cor. 13:8). This is how I begin to love *God* by loving another. This is how the two commandments come together in such correlation and union.

When my heart is moved in love for another, when I take that leap that only love can lead to, *then* is my love for God demonstrated. When in lowliness of heart, I enter into the mind of Christ that truly esteems others better than myself, pursuing the interests of others and not just my own, *then* does He receive from me love of the highest measure (Phil. 2:3–5; Jn. 15:12; 1 Jn. 3:16).

Highest Love, Greatest Joy

Jesus peers into the deep places of our hearts as His words ring throughout the corridors of timelessness, "'Love one another as I have loved you'" (Jn. 13:34). With His ageless love, He urges the one who loves Him to love in the way that *Love loves*, to love in the way that He has eternally loved, to lay down his life on behalf of others, to give everything for love and to hold nothing back.

Jesus implores, "'Greater love has no one than this, than to lay down one's life for his friends. You are My friends if you do what I command you…'" (Jn. 15:12–14). With these words He says in essence, "Love each other with the deep sacrifice and abandonment that I have loved you with—the very same love. In the laying down of your life entirely for another, you will enter the greatest love of highest heights. This is how I have eternally loved, and this is how I invite you, as my friends, to show your friendship with Me. Love one another."

As these two commands converge in our hearts and lives, becoming one river of a continual offering of love unto God, we will begin to live in the pleasures of what Jesus described as joy made full (Jn. 15:11). We will find joy as each activity is done in love; each word spoken is uttered as though unto God; each service rendered is crowned with the dignity of being done from the heart. Touching the existence that in truth is the only way to live, we will enter into that kind of abiding, never departing, always continuing in love. And in such living, the Lord Jesus will answer our cry as He has promised by manifesting Himself to us. He will look upon the entirety of our response in love, the embracing of His commands to love Him wholly and to love others in the same way, and He and the Father will come to us and make Their home with us (Jn. 14:21, 23).

The supreme place of love is in the yielding and emptying of itself. In the actions of laying down our lives for our spouses, our families, our friends, and even our enemies, there we find the highest heights of communion with the One whose nature has eternally been to lay Himself down for the cause of love. As we give everything, just as He has given everything, loving others as He has loved us, we abide in love and enter into the fullness of joy—joy inexpressible and full of glory (Jn. 15:11; 1 Pet. 1:8).

Closing Prayer

O God, we desire to respond to Your invitation to *love* You with all that we are….to lay down our lives for others as our expression and demonstration of love for You. O You, who take a weak heart and bring forth a love unyielding, lay hold of our hearts with jealousy. Awaken in us a holy givenness that is not just periodic but *perpetual.* Move us into the place where we are looking for You, finding signs of Your love in the everyday and responding amidst ordinary activities with extraordinary love. Oh, that we would love You with all that we are, and that nothing would be found lacking as everything is given. As You have loved us, may we love You, giving all as You have given all—fully and with our *entirety.*

ORDER INFORMATION

US orders go to: www.danacandler.com.
For volume discounts, visit the web site.
For orders outside US visit: www.ihop.org (see bookstore)

ADDITIONAL PRODUCT

BOOKS

Deep unto Deep: the Journey of His Embrace

Rewards of Fasting

Way of Intimacy Study Guide

MUSIC

Deep unto Deep Instrumental CD & Study Guide

CD AUDIO TEACHINGS

Love Gives All (2 Teachings)

Deep unto Deep (6 Teachings)

Fasting: Rewards and Perils (5 Teachings)

Song of Solomon Overview (2 Teachings)

ABOUT THE AUTHOR

Dana Candler resides in Kansas City, Missouri with her husband Matt and their two children. Serving as intercessory missionaries at the International House of Prayer, Matt and Dana have been a part of the leadership team since IHOP began in 1999. Dana is the author of *Deep unto Deep* and Co-Author with Mike Bickle of *Rewards of Fasting*. She is also an instructor at the Forerunner School of Ministry, a full-time Bible school affiliated with the International House of Prayer.

The passion of Dana's heart is the subject of deep intimacy with God and the unending quest for the fullness of His love that we were each created for. Intensifying this passion is her burden regarding the urgency of this present hour of history and the desperate need for believers everywhere to become fully alive in the realm of love—that they might be fully prepared for the culminating events before Christ's return.

THE INTERNATIONAL
HOUSE OF PRAYER OF KANSAS CITY

On September 19, 1999, a prayer meeting began in Kansas City that continues to this day. From dawn till dusk and throughout the watches of the night, prayer and worship continues twenty-four hours a day, seven days a week. The Prayer Room is the heartbeat—the essence and origin—of all that goes on at the the International House of Prayer. This 24-hour, citywide, inter-denominational prayer ministry is modeled after the Tabernacle of David (1 Chr. 13–16; 23–25) and focused on the "prayer side" of the Great Commission. It is based on the reality that worship, music and intercession flow together in heaven around God's Throne (Rev. 4–5). The Scripture prophesies that God will again raise up the Tabernacle of David in the context of gathering the Great Harvest of new believers at the end of the age (Acts 15:16; Amos 9:11). This implies a dynamic world-wide "intercessory worship" movement that will be in full force during the generation in which the Lord returns.

Convinced that Jesus is worthy of incessant ado-ration, men and women of all ages from across the globe are giving themselves to extravagant love expressed through 24/7 prayer. Structured in 84 two-hour meetings a week, full teams of musicians, singers, and intercessors (missionaries) lift their voices in praise and supplication, asking God to fulfill His promise and give the nations of the earth to Jesus as His inheritance. May the fire on the altar never go out.

For more info on the International House of Prayer visit www.ihop.org.